EDUCATION IN CHANGING INDIAN SOCIETY

– Philosophical Aspect

Dr. Urmila Sampat
Dr. Shakuntala Gayatonde
Mrs. Sharda Ganapathy

Hansraj Jivandas College of Education,
Khar (W),
Mumbai - 400 052.

Himalaya Publishing House

• Mumbai • New Delhi • Nagpur • Bengaluru • Hyderabad
• Chennai • Pune • Lucknow • Ahmedabad • Ernakulam
• Bhubaneswar • Indore • Kolkata • Guwahati

First Edition : 1996
Reprint : 1997
Reprint : 2007
Reprint : 2011
Reprint : 2013

Published by : Mrs. Meena Pandey for **Himalaya Publishing House Pvt. Ltd.**, "Ramdoot", Dr. Bhalerao Marg, Girgaon, **Mumbai - 400 004.** Phone: 022-23860170/23863863, Fax: 022-23877178 **E-mail: himpub@vsnl.com; Website: www.himpub.com**

Branch Offices :

New Delhi : "Pooja Apartments", 4-B, Murari Lal Street, Ansari Road, Darya Ganj, New Delhi - 110 002. Phone: 011-23270392, 23278631; Fax: 011-23256286

Nagpur : Kundanlal Chandak Industrial Estate, Ghat Road, Nagpur - 440 018. Phone: 0712-2738731, 3296733; Telefax: 0712-2721216

Bengaluru : No. 16/1 (Old 12/1), 1st Floor, Next to Hotel Highlands, Madhava Nagar, Race Course Road, Bengaluru - 560 001. Phone: 080-22286611, 22385461, 4113 8821, 22281541

Hyderabad : No. 3-4-184, Lingampally, Besides Raghavendra Swamy Matham, Kachiguda, Hyderabad - 500 027. Phone: 040-27560041, 27550139

Chennai : 8/2 Madley 2nd street, T. Nagar, Chennai - 600 017. Mobile: 09320490962

Pune : First Floor, "Laksha" Apartment, No. 527, Mehunpura, Shaniwarpeth (Near Prabhat Theatre), Pune - 411 030. Phone: 020-24496323/24496333; Mobile: 09370579333

Lucknow : House No 731, Shekhupura Colony, Near B.D. Convent School, Aliganj, Lucknow - 226 022. Phone: 0522-4012353; Mobile: 09307501549

Ahmedabad : 114, "SHAIL", 1st Floor, Opp. Madhu Sudan House, C.G. Road, Navrang Pura, Ahmedabad - 380 009. Phone: 079-26560126; Mobile: 09377088847

Ernakulam : 39/104 A, Lakshmi Apartment, Karikkamuri Cross Rd., Ernakulam, Cochin - 622011, Kerala. Phone: 0484-2378012, 2378016; Mobile: 09387122121

Bhubaneswar : 5 Station Square, Bhubaneswar - 751 001 (Odisha). Phone: 0674-2532129, Mobile: 09338746007

Indore : Kesardeep Avenue Extension, 73, Narayan Bagh, Flat No. 302, IIIrd Floor, Near Humpty Dumpty School, Indore - 452 007 (M.P.). Mobile: 09303399304

Kolkata : 108/4, Beliaghata Main Road, Near ID Hospital, Opp. SBI Bank, Kolkata - 700 010, Phone: 033-32449649, Mobile: 7439040301

Guwahati : House No. 15, Behind Pragjyotish College, Near Sharma Printing Press, O. Bharalumukh, Guwahati - 781009, (Assam). Mobile: 09883055590, 08486355289, 7439040301

Printed at : Rose Fine Art, Mumbai. On behalf of HPH.

PREFACE

"*Education pulsates life from all corners, awakens the mind fully, allows one to manifest and fillips one to be perfect.*"

As Rabindranath Tagore states, '*Education stimulates the spirit within, awakens consciousness and radiates into the thoughts and actions of the individual.*' Therefore Educational Philosophy is basically or fundamentally the way of life, primarily of the individual and of the society at large. It is the sum-total of the beliefs, attitudes and thoughts reflected in the behaviour of the individual.

We, the teacher-educators, teaching the subject for a number of years, felt that students were always unnecessarily terrorised by the very title Educational Philosophy. It was considered to be as something abstract and incomprehensible and totally beyond the purview of student-community. Since then, it has always been our endeavour to make our students realise that philosophy is only a way of life and quest for knowledge. Educational Philosophy is only an understanding of the concepts and theories underlying the practice of education.

With a deep sense of gratitude, we thank our librarian, Mrs. L. V. Nayampally, who has helped us in going through the manuscript and making valuable suggestions.

We hope this book will be useful to students and bring a change in their attitude to philosophy.

Dr. Urmi Sampat
Dr. Shakuntala Gayatonde
Sharada Ganapathy

CONTENTS

1

EDUCATION

- ☞ *Meaning*
- ☞ *Definitions*
- ☞ *Characteristics*

"Education is not a luxury which can be afforded after development has occured. It is an integral part, an inescapable and essential part of the development itself." **Dean Rusk**

Preamble

Education is a joyful experience. In fact, education at its best is ecstatic. It is the skillful pursuit of excellence. At its best, it is most effective, and the moment of learning becomes a moment of delight.

Education is an integral part of every individual's life. It is a process that changes the learner. It helps to make the right kind of choice and have a clear conception of the social world. Every individual perceives it in the light of his own experience. The successful professional views it as the key to success. An ardent learner takes recourse to it as an eternal fountain head to quench his thirst for knowledge.

There are many more concepts arising out of perception, coloured by the angle from which it is viewed. It is the role of the educationists and teachers to understand the concept to its very core and work as a team for the reconstruction of education, device new strategies and open new avenues to cater to the expectations and aspirations of all age-groups from diverse strategies of society. With this preamble, we begin our ramble to gather the wealth of education in all its manifestations

Importance of Education

From times immemorial, Man has utilised his power of speech to communicate with other individuals and transmit a store of practical experiences from group to group, from generation to generation. The resources for this communication were mainly individual memories and the means of communication was chiefly oral. Knowledge is power — as indicated by this aphorism, a learned person was held in great esteem throughout the world. Education, in its original sense means acquiring knowledge and learning. In this context, it is interesting to analyse what motivates an individual to get education.

Education was a biological necessity for the primitive Man. The need to protect himself from the hazards of his environment motivated him to understand his environment and to fulfil his biological need of food, shelter and clothing.

Human faculties and potentialities will develop only if the proper stimulus and congenial environment are provided. A deaf and mute person cannot develop the mental faculties of a child to the fullest. Education through the development of mental faculties is a biological necessity. This development of mental faculties can be achieved by satisfaction and sublimation of instincts.

While struggling with his environmental conditions, Man organised himself gradually and created his society for group endeavour in the form of family units and tribes. As a group greater concentration was on vital material tasks. During this process, knowledge and experience were acquired and the capacity to express desires and aspirations was developed. This resulted in the defining and fashioning of his mental faculties.

As the various civilisations developed, Education was influenced by the historical and political development, customs and traditions.

Since the Second World War, Education constitutes a vital component in any effort for development and human progress. It plays a dominant role in the formulation of national and international policies.

A human being is endowed with higher mental faculties such as thinking, reasoning, imagination and creativity. These potentialities need to be developed through appropriate learning experiences and education. So Education helps in the development of the personality of the individual.

Education foresees and prepares individuals for a future society striving hard to cope up with accelerated development, ever changing trends and to cater to the needs of an expanding learning society.

We are on the threshold of a technocratic and electronic age. The greatest need of the day is to provide education which would produce individuals with a high degree of technical skills with creative and innovative abilities that would enable them to face the challenges of the future. Creation of awareness on various aspects of life is essential to improve the quality of life of the individual and society. This type of awareness enables them to tackle the problems of population explosion and environmental deterioration.

Thus Education assumes a colossal importance and needs to be of the status of a national movement.

Meaning of Education

Education is a dynamic process which enables man to grow, develop, adjust and adapt to accelerated change. It is a complex process, conditioned by multi-dimensional factors. Hence there are diverse opinions regarding the derivation and definition of the term 'Education'.

Etymology of the word 'Education'

Educare — Latin word meaning to bring up or to nourish, *E* out and *ducere* to lead out or draw out. Hence education means to lead out or to draw out.

Educatum — Latin word meaning act of teaching or training.

From all these derivations, it may be stated that Education denotes

- acquisition of knowledge and experiences
- development of skills, habits and attitudes
- a process of training which provides a variety of experiences and thus draws out the best of the individual.

Considering the Sanskrit word for Education, the commonly known word is '*shiksha*' which is derived from the word '*shas*' which means *to discipline.* The word '*vidya*' which denotes the subject matter of the body of knowledge is derived from the verb root '*vid*' *to know.* Hence according to the Indian derivation, there is greater emphasis on imparting knowledge by disciplining the mind through various branches of knowledge.

Definition of Education

The connotation of Education has differed according to the specific emphasis laid by different thinkers. The emphasis has been changing from time to time. Therefore some of the definitions which reflect the transformations the concept has gone through are discussed under the following heads:

- *Indian Concept of Education*
- *Western Concept of Education*
- *Modern Concept of Education*

Indian Concept of Education

The following are some of the definitions of Education according to the Indian Concept:

"Education is something which makes man self-reliant self-less."

— Rig Veda

"Education is that whose end product is salvation."

— Upanishads

"Human Education means the training which one gets from nature."

— Panini

"Education means training for the country and love for the nation."

— Kautilya

In these definitions, the ideals of Ancient Indian Education are reflected as follows:

- *inculcation of values*
- *development of the individual and his contribution to the country*
- *education helps in liberation*

In order to understand the concept of Education according to the later Indian educators some of the definitions are presented here. They are as follows:

"Education is self-realisation and service of the people."

— Guru Nanak

"Education is the manifestation of divine perfection, already existing in Man."

— Swami Vivekananda

"Education means enabling the mind to find out the ultimate truth which emancipates us from the garbage of the dust and gives us the wealth, not of things but of inner control, not of power but of love, making this truth its own and giving a mission to it."

— Rabindranath Tagore

"Education means helping the growing soul to draw out that which is in itself."

— Aurobindo Ghose

"By Education, I mean an all round drawing out of the best in child and man — body, mind and spirit."

— Mahatma Gandhi

"Education is the process of the individual mind getting to its full possible development. It is a long school, which lasts a life time."

— Zakir Hussain

A study of these definitions indicates that the aspects emphasised are as follows:

- *complete development of the personality*
- *enrichment of the subtle aspects of his mind*

Western Concept of Education

Having understood the fundamental characteristics of education as reflected by the definitions given by Indian thinkers, let us proceed to discuss the definitions of education given by Western Philosophers.

"Education is the capacity to feel pleasure and pain at the right moment. It develops in the body and in the soul of the pupils, the beauty and all the perfection which he is capable of."

— Plato

"Education is the creation of a sound mind in a sound body."

— Aristotle

"Education is a natural, harmonious and progressive development of man's innate powers."

Pestalozzi

"Education is the complete development of the individuality of the child so that he can make an original contribution of human life, according to the best of his capacity."

— T. P. Nunn

"Education is the process of living through continuous reconstruction of experiences."

— John Dewey

"Education is the deliberate and systematic influence exerted by the mature person upon the immature through instruction, discipline and harmonious development of physical, intellectual, aesthetic, social and spiritual powers of human being according to individual and social needs and directed towards the union of the educand with the creator as the final end."

— Redden

"Education we receive from three sources - Nature, men and things. Spontaneous development of our organs and capacities constitute the education of nature."

— Rousseau

A study of these definitions indicates that not only is the individual's personality but the social interaction and experiences of life out of which education is the outcome are also given importance.

Modern Concept of Education

Education is the single enterprise in developing countries. It is a key to more rapid and more meaningful economic growth.

Dr. Radhakrishnan stated "A new world society is gradually emerging. It is growing quietly, imperceptibly in the minds and hearts of men. The tumult and excitement, the anger and the violence, the perplexities of the spirit and the ambiguities of expression are the pangs of the birth of something new. We, of the generation are called upon to work for the new order, with all the strength and capacity for suffering we possess."

These words indicate the ushering in of a new world society with changing needs, aspirations and expectations. Educational change and social change must take place simultaneously. The classroom, as envisaged by Prof. Ram Joshi is the place where the entire human culture is in a melting pot. Education is the most important factor in achieving rapid economic development through technological development and in creating a social order based on the values of freedom, social justice and equal responsibility. Education plays a vital role in the building of an active learning society. It is the total transformation of man.

The main thrusts of Education are development of the mental faculties of man, his skills of learning and provision of vocational training. A great revolution in Education is needed to achieve the greatly desired social, economic and cultural revolution. Educational change and social change must be at par. The process of change can be facilitated by education by playing a liberating and renovating role, by examining and analysing the existing social situation and posing an alternative ideology to remedy the limitations of an existing ideology. An educational revolution is a must to bring about social change.

Before discussing the characteristics and salient features of Education, it is essential to differentiate the term 'Education' from the narrower concepts with which it is confused.

1. Education and Instruction\Teaching

Instruction\Teaching means imparting knowledge of a particular subject in a systematic, planned, logical way. Education implies acquisition of knowledge and experience as well as development of skills, habits and attitudes which help a person to lead a full and happy life. It is complete development of a student's personality.

2. Education and Training

Training is formal and involves supervision and framework of rules and regulations. Education may be given formally as well as informally.

3. Education and Schooling

Schooling is a wider term than instruction as it includes curricular and co-curricular activities. Education is not confined to a particular period but it is a life-long process.

4. Education and Literacy

Literacy is just a means by which a man or woman can be educated. It is neither the beginning nor the end of education. Education is an all-round harmonious development of personality.

5. Education and Information

Information is useful for education but education is much wider than mere collection of information.

Characteristics of Education

(i) Education is not co-terminus with Institutional Education

Institutional Education or Formal Education means education imparted in the school. This is a very narrow concept of education which is minimal compared to the various agencies like family, society and mass media which infulence the child from the time of birth.

(ii) Education is a life long process

The package of Education given at the school or college is not adequate as what is learnt yesterday becomes out-dated today owing to knowledge explosion. As a result of this, there is always a challenge before the individual to keep abreast of the latest development not only in his field but on the whole. An individual cannot afford to remain complacent with one skill or one branch alone. It is necessary for an individual to be acquainted with other branches of knowledge also. For this, it is incumbent on the individual to be a life-long learner.

(iii) Education brings about integrated development of the individual

The child develops and grows as a result of nourishment and maturation. As a child develops physically, training is necessary to develop the mental faculties. In this process, it is absolutely essential that the emotional needs of the child are satisfied to ensure his healthy emotional development. The school plays a dominant role in the socialisation of the child and consequently on his social development. Therefore, as defined by Redden, the mature person influences the immature person systematically and in a planned manner and brings about a balanced and harmonious development of the individual.

(iv) Education is a tri-polar process

Education is the process which evolves out of the interaction of the educator and the educand. Hence it was considered to be a bipolar process. As a result of the emphasis laid on the sociological aspect of Education by John Dewey, Education was considered to be a tripolar process. *The three vertices of the triangle are Educator, Educand and Society* i.e. the teacher who imparts education, the pupil who receives it and the social milieu or the social environment in which Education is imparted.

(v) Education is need-based

The individual is a member of Society and contributes to the development of the Society. Education, therefore provides the Manpower for national development. In order to achieve the development of the individual and his potential, education has to cater to the needs of the individual. The social structure is becoming more complex and diverse. Therefore, education has to be dynamic, flexible and pragmatic to cope not only with the present situation but also with the changes that are likely to take place in the future.

Hence education must cater not only to the capacities and abilities of the individual but also to the social, economic and physical needs of the community for whom it is meant. It should reflect the culture, traditions and values, attitudes, interests and needs of the society. It helps the future generation to adapt to the changing situations.

(vi) Education is a transmitter and preserver of culture

Society is constantly progressing from the past to the future. The traditions and culture provide the basis for the developing society. The experiences of the past enrich the society and enable it to lay the foundations of the future. As Brown says "*Education brings about change in behaviour and if its main functions are to remain as mere transmission of culture, it will fall short of its role in a dynamic society.*" Education must also provide situations at all age levels, but within the maturity and ability of the individual, to stimulate creativeness of mind, which can explore new horizons and bring the vision of future into reality. Theory and practice of Education are influenced by social change. In the present democratic set up group dynamics, inculcation of values, development of creativity and citizenship have to be given priority.

(vii) Education should be relevant to life situations

Education can be of any utility only if it has relevance to life. Education has to be practical and realistic and not theoretical and bookish. Education has to be skill-based and job-oriented to enable the individual to become self-reliant and self-sufficient.

(viii) Education plays a dominant role in Human Resource Development through Manpower Planning

Economic development of a nation depends on how efficiently the human resources are developed. Human Resource Development can be achieved only if it is based on effective Manpower Planning. Manpower Planning ensures that the manpower, that is, the appropriate type of personnel are generated and nurtured, bearing in mind the urban and rural requirements of the Nation — namely industries and agriculture.

Human Resource Development is the process of increasing the knowledge, the skills and capacities of all people in society. According to *Economics*, Human Resource Development means accumulation of human capital and its effective investment in the development of an economy. In *political* terms, Human Resource Development prepares people for active participation in political processes, particularly as citizens in a democracy. From the *social and cultural* point of view, the development of human resources helps people to lead fuller and richer lives, less bound by tradition. The process of Human Resource Development unlocks the door to modernisation.

Human resources are developed by formal education, on-the-job informal training programs and institutionalised adult education programs. Two other processes of Human Resource Development are improvements in the health of the working population through medical facilities and health programs, and improvement in nutrition which increase the working capacity of the people. *Alfred Marshall emphasised the importance of Education as a national investment and in his view the most valuable of all capital is that invested in human beings.*

The objective of a strategy of Human Resource Development is to build the skills and knowledge required for economic, social, cultural and political growth and to provide avenues of participation in the creation of a better society for all.

SUMMARY

1. Importance of Education.

i. Education — a biological necessity to protect himself.

ii. Education and development of mental faculties essential for man who is coping with developing trends and resultant change.

iii. Education needed for producing individuals with high technical abilities in an electronic age.

2. Meaning of Education.

i. Etymological : 'Educare' to nourish to bring up 'E' out 'ducere' to lead 'Educatum' act of teaching or training

ii. Education denotes

- acquisition of knowledge and experience
- development of skills, habits and attitudes
- process of training which provides a variety of experiences and there by drawing out the best of the individual.

3. Definitions of Education.

Indian Concept

- Ancient Indian Education emphasise on

(i) inculcation of values,

(ii) development of the individual,

(iii) complete development of the individual's personality.

Western Concept

The development of personality, social interaction and experiences of life are emphasised.

Modern Concept

Revolution and change brought about by Education.

EDUCATION IS NOT TEACHING, INSTRUCTION, TRAINING, LITERACY SCHOOLING.

4. Characteristics of Education

i. Education is a life-long process.

ii. Education brings about integrated development.

iii. Education is a tripolar process.

iv. Education is need-based.

v. Education is transmitter and preserver of culture.

vi. Education is life-oriented.

vii. Education plays a dominant role in Human Resource Development and Manpower Planning.

2

SCOPE OF EDUCATION

- *Relation with other disciplines*
- *Areas of Education*
- *Types of Education*

"Education is a practical art, which draw on many theoretical disciplines — the humanities, the social and biological sciences. Education is a co-operative rather than an operative art."

Houle

Introduction

Education is a wide and vast subject with its roots in many disciplines and extending widely to cover and contribute to many fields. So the scope of education is multi-faceted and multi-disciplinary blending into one enterprise to achieve the individual and national development.

SCOPE OF EDUCATION

The facets of the scope of education are as follows:

(i) Relation with other disciplines

(ii) Areas of education

(iii) Types of education

(i) Relation with other disciplines

Education is both a science and an art. Education has a broad-based foundation built with the bricks of the basic principles of other disciplines. Consequently the principles of

Education and other disciplines are closely interwoven into the fabric of the educational system. The disciplines with which Education is linked are the following:

- Philosophy
- Psychology
- Sociology
- Economics
- Politics
- Biology

Having understood the fact that Education and other disciplines are inter-related, let us see how each of the disciplines have contributed to Education.

Philosophy

Philosophy is a love for knowledge and a quest for truth. This quest for truth is conducted with the help of the five branches. They are as under:

Logic: the study of the process of thinking

Ethics: the theory of morality

Aesthetics: science of beauty

Epistemology: the theory of knowledge and

Metaphysics: nature of reality

These methods, knowingly or unknowingly, are utilised by all of us in our attempt to understand and adapt to our environment and solve our daily problems. The concepts and theories evolving out of these method's form the body of knowledge, i.e. content of all disciplines. These concepts and theories enable us to analyse and comprehend the natural phenomena, establish relationships and learn constantly from our experiences, communicate these to others and share our pleasure and pain with our fellow-beings with love, sense of belongingness, commitment and co-operation and co-existence. Generally, Philosophy is considered to be abstract, vague and incomprehensible. It is even described *as searching for a black cat in a dark room.* These are all misconceptions. As Raymont states "*Philosophy is an increasing effort to discover the general truth that lies behind the particular facts, to discern the reality that lies behind appearance.*"

Philosophy is the Queen of all Sciences. It is the fusion of all the sciences and arts. In fact this is the reason why the highest degree in any field is termed as Ph.D or Doctor of Philosophy. Philosophy is an integral part of our life. The philosophy of life of a person is reflected in the way he thinks, his attitude to life as reflected in his values and the way he acts or behaves. For example, even if we observe how two individuals react to the same situation we can understand their philosophy. So Philosophy gives us the principles of life, guides our relationships, concretises our perceptions and enables us to interpret our experiences.

Education is life-oriented, need-based and develops the personality of the individual to the maximum potential. It is a lifelong process. Philosophy provides the fundamental principles of Education and Education implements these principles through its practicum. Philosophy is the contemplative aspect and Education is the practical aspect. Education is the dynamic side of Philosophy. So Education and Philosophy are the two sides of the same coin. Consequently, fusion of Education and Philosophy has resulted in the branch of Education known as *Educational Philosophy.*

Educational Philosophy or The Philosophical Foundations of Education deals with the principles of Philosophy which have influenced the various aspects of Education, namely, the *concept of Education, Aims, Curriculum, Textbook, Discipline, Role of the Teacher, Methods of Teaching and Techniques of Evaluation.* The schools of Philosophy and the educational ideas of great philosophers have influenced the educational policies and practices.

Psychology

Psychology is a study of human behaviour in relation to his environment. Psychological theories and concepts enable the educationist to plan and formulate the policies and decide upon the educational practices. For example, the stages of growth and development, and the concept of individual differences guide the curriculum designing, selection of the content, writing of instructional objectives, organisation of the teaching programme and selection and provision of appropriate learning experiences. Psychology enables the teacher to understand the behaviour of children and their problems and tackle them effectively.

Educational Psychology is Psychology as applied to Education. Learner-centred Education makes the learner the focal point of education. Educational Psychology facilitates application of theories of Learning, Cognitive Development, Concept Formation to the educational situations. It provides the guidelines for achieving Human Resource Development with excellence, creativity and innovation.

Sociology

Sociology is the study of society. The structure of society, the family pattern, the social institutions, economic order and the needs and aspirations of society are the principles of sociology which govern the social aspect of education. *School is a miniature society* and the process of socialisation of the individual begins at school. The teacher is the social engineer who attempts to bring about social change through her students and their parents with whom she has constant relationship and interaction. It is therefore essential that the teacher has a thorough understanding of society and the students she is moulding and tailoring to the needs of the society. Thus the branch of Educational Sociology became an important area of education.

Educational Sociology is Sociology applied to Education. Educational Sociology is the basis of social development. It analyses the role of education in a changing emerging society. It establishes a cooperative linkage between educational institutions, social and voluntary organisations and other agencies of education. It provides an opportunity for people's actions by creating social awareness among the various strata of society. Conscientisation and Problematisation through group discussion is the application of Educational Sociology. The functions of education, namely, conservation and transmission of culture and values, eradicating traditionalism and progressing towards rationalism are made possible by Educational Sociology.

Biology

Biology is the study of living organisms. The structure of the human body as differentiated from the animals, that is, the erect posture, the arms and the capacities of the fingers provide useful facts for the aspect of skill-development in Education. The milestones of physical development and maturation of human beings are the foundations of physical education, pre-primary education and primary education. They provide guidelines for planning educational activities.

The theories regarding nutrients, proteins and other essential components of a balanced diet contribute greatly towards the quality of education. This quality of education is achieved by creating an awareness among the educationists regarding the impact of lack of complete nutrition on the educational achievement of the pupils.

The Fundamental biological laws of rest and fatigue are the basic principles of planning a good educational programme. The principles of genetic engineering enable teachers and educationists to identify biological problems in children and adopt appropriate remedial measures. Thus, though there is no area of education as Educational Biology, Biology and Education have to work in coordination to develop a physically and mentally healthy achieving society.

Economics

One of the major functions of education is achieving economic development of the individual and society. Therefore, Economics contributes the concept of economic order, consumer awareness, production and marketing to education. It directs the financial policies of education. Decisions regarding the cost effectiveness, allocations for various levels of education are guided by the principles of economics. All these constitutes the area of Economics of Education.

Politics

Political systems have influenced the theory and practice of education from the very beginning. Education gets its direction from the political systems. For example, the National Policy on Education, 1986, was suggested and initiated by the Congress Government and later on in 1990 changes in government policy led to the appointment of the Rammurthi Committee to review the National Policy on Education. The National Policy for women and policies regarding women's education has gained top priority owing to the influence of political activists. Political theories, if viewed in the right perspectives should help in averting the ill effects of politicisation. Contrarily, the mal-effects of political exploitation have led to many mal-practices. So education has to be used to the fullest capacity to protect Human Rights by creating political awareness in society. The influence of politics has been instrumental in educating the people to fight against exploitation, injustice and to protect their Human Rights as an individual and as a consumer.

(ii) Areas of Education

So far we have understood how the various disciplines have enriched the concept of education and enlivened the practice of education. We now proceed to the areas of education which have furnished the subject matter for various studies in education. These areas also comprise of the issues in education, problems in education and developing trends in education. The areas are the following:

1. Educational Philosophy
2. Educational Psychology
3. Educational Sociology
4. Economics of Education
5. Politics of Education
6. History of Education
7. Comparative Education
8. Problems of Education
9. Educational Management
10. Educational Technology
11. Research in Education

Out of these areas, the first five have been dealt with in the earlier sub-section on relation with other disciplines. Now we proceed to deal with the *major areas of education.*

History of Education

It records the stages in the development of education in relation with the different periods in history. It enables one to understand the various political conditions and ideologies that have influenced the system of education. Thus it helps in evolving an appropriate educational system according to the needs and changes in the society.

Comparative Education

It is the study of the educational systems of various countries with a view to facilitating the comparison of the structure, operation, aims, methods, practices of different countries and achievements of various systems of education. Thus Comparative Education enables educationists to reconstruct, restructure, and reform education.

Problems of Education

Issues in education in other words cover a wide range and are of a diverse nature. The issues are complex and need to be tackled with insight and foresight. Some of the problems are over-crowded classrooms, education for all, special education, teaching the disadvantaged, administration, problems of universalisation of elementary education, equalisation of educational opportunities. examination reform, vocational and technical education and women's education. Attempts are constantly being made to study these problems in depth, analyse them and tackle them in the best possible manner.

Educational Management

It is one of the major factors which determine the effectiveness of the entire educational system. The quality of education depends on the fundamental principles and the dynamic nature of its components, the meaningfulness of the goals, relevance of the curricular and co-curricular activities, the effectiveness of instruction, skill development, empowerment of work force, human resource development, monitoring and evaluation of the organisational climate.

Educational Technology

It is the pivot of the cost-effectiveness of education. The process of teaching opens a number of avenues for diversity of learning experience, effective stimulus variation, teaching, learning strategies, use of appropriate audio-visual material, efficient use of hardware and software and creative use of innovative techniques in education.

Research in Education

Just as R & D (i.e.Research and Development) is the key to industrial progress, similarly in the field of education, research lays the foundations of educational excellence. Developing trends open new avenues for Research and

Development. Some of the topics in which studies can be conducted are:

- *Non-formal Education*
- *Adult Education*
- *Technical Education*
- *Vocationalisation of Education*
- *Women's Education*
- *Action Research for improving the Quality of Education*
- *Diagnostic and Remedial teaching*
- *Measurement and Evaluation*

Besides the interdisciplinary approaches which lead to the diverse branches of education, the scope of education extends beyond formal to informal and non-formal education. It concerns itself with the multi-dimensional approach and reaching out to the remotest corner of the world through Distance Education, Open Schools and Universities. The information technology has widened the horizons of education and made education ever-widening in its scope to encompass the developing trends and innovative practices.

(iii) Types of Education

Education has multifarious functions to perform. These functions cannot be fulfilled with a single approach. Hence, different strategies and different approaches have to be adopted in order to cater to various stages of life, multiple-educational needs and aspirations, and variety of problems confronting the economically and socially disadvantaged. Consequently, types of education have been evolved based on the fundamental concepts and characteristics of education.

Concept of Lifelong Education

Lifelong Education connotes education which continues through life. The concept of lifelong education has been the fulcrum of Ancient Education. It is a very old concept but it has come to the fore and developed into a major principle due to the obsolescence of the existing knowledge arising out of knowledge explosion and fast developing trends in every field. Besides, the need for improvement of the quality of life has been realised. Lifelong Education is a solution to the growing demands of the world.

The needs of the world which necessitate improvement of the quality of life through the concept of lifelong education are as follows:

- Change in social roles confronted by the individual right from infancy to the end of life,
- Psychological growth and change occuring at different stages of life,
- Social, economic, cultural needs and those needs pertaining to the inner personal life that necessitate acquisition of new skills, knowledge, attitude and relearning or even unlearning of what was acquired before.

A realisation of these needs motivated the International Commission on Development of Education and UNESCO, Hamburg, to discuss, enunciate and evolve the concept of lifelong education. Various projects were undertaken and completed by various countries. On the basis of the reports of the projects and deliberations at the International Conferences organised by UNESCO, a report Learning to Be edited by Edgar Faure was brought out in 1972 and a later report Education on the move was published in 1976.

The fundamental principles underlying the concept of Lifelong Education are as follows:

- Lifelong Education is co-extensive and co-terminus with life.
- Education will be multi-dimensional, multi-media and multi-source so that closed teaching systems can be transformed into open learning systems.
- Freedom and Flexibility are to be ensured in the learning system.
- It views education as a totality and unifies all stages of education.
- It includes formal, non-formal as well as incidental or informal learning.
- The process of lifelong education is initiated in the home. Community plays an important role in the system of lifelong education.

- It is universal in character signifying democratisation of education and equalisation of educational opportunities.
- It is dynamic in approach allowing adaptation of material and alternative patterns of acquiring education.
- The three major pre-requisites of lifelong education are:
  1. opportunity i.e. a rich educative environment
  2. motivation i.e. a strong desire to learn and
  3. educability i.e. the readiness to profit from learning opportunities.

The outcome of the processes of Lifelong Education is an emerging Learning Society which is a product of an open learning system and teachers throughout the society, that is, any member of society, who has expertise in any branch can become a teacher of that branch even though the person may not have any specific qualifications of the faculty of Education.

The processes of Lifelong Education have evolved into the various types of education —

(1) Formal Education,

(2) Non-Formal Education and

(3) Informal Education.

Formal Education

Formal Education means structural education. According to the Dictionary of Education by Carter V. Good, *Formal Education is any training or education that is conventional, given in an orderly, logical, planned and systematic manner.* Dr.Philip Coombs defines *Formal Education as one which is given through formal institutions like school, college or university.* It is the traditional system in which the teacher and the taught face each other in a classroom situation on a regular and continuous basis, follow a fixed and pre-determined syllabus, secure promotion to the next class after passing the previous class, take a public examination at the end of the course, and receive a certificate, diploma or degree. The formal system of education is a single point entry, sequential and full-time system of instruction. It connotes rigid adherence to rules.

Non-Formal Education

Non-Formal Education is an alternative strategy of education envisaged to provide opportunities of education for those who have been deprived of it and those who are not in a position to attend to full-time formal course.The present context where Education for all is the main goal to be achieved, Non-Formal Education has a great relevance and a dominant role to play.

The salient features of Non-Formal Education are as follows:

- deliberately planned clear goals and well-defined programmes
- oriented flexibly in terms of learner, life and environment
- diversified content and method
- non-authoritarian
- built-in learner participation
- mobilisation of local resources
- enrichment of human and environmental potential
- no age bar or need of previous qualification

Informal Education

The term informal education is defined by Philips Coombs and Mansoor Ahmed as the process by which a person imbibes attitudes, develops skills, cultivates values and acquires knowledge without there being an organisation or system about it. Informal Education denotes all incidental learning that takes place at work or play or during travels. Informal Education is without formality and without form. It is unstructured, spontaneous or incidental.

Formal, Non-Formal and Informal Education cannot afford to be seperate entities, totally isolated from one another. Education will have to be viewed holistically. The pattern of education with a futuristic approach will have to be of a flexible nature emphasising non-institutionalised and open-entry structures, thereby signifying synthesis of all the three types of education.

Thus it may be stated that the scope of education is as vast as the skies and fathoms deep like the ocean full with the gems of knowledge of a variety of disciplines with a diversity of approaches and rich mineral wealth to explore through Researches in Education. Thereby, it reflects the universality and diversity of the Scope of Education.

SUMMARY

Scope of Education:

(i) Relation with other disciplines:

Philosophy, Psychology, Sociology. Economics, Politics and Biology.

(ii) Areas of Education:

Educational Philosophy, Educational Psychology, Educational Sociology, Economics of Education, Politics of Education, History of Education, Comparative Education, Problems of Education, Educational Management, Educational Technology and Research in Education.

(iii) Types of Education:

Concept of Lifelong Education - evolved into various types of education — Formal, Non-Formal and Informal Education.

3

FUNCTIONS OF EDUCATION

☞ *A. Functions of Education in the development of the individual*
☞ *B. Role of Education in National Development*

Education is an investment in people. Through education we nurture the abilities of the child and extend those in the individual. **—*Theodore Schulz***

Education by its very nature looks to the future and prepares for it. It is of universal interest and concerns everybody. The role of education is to contribute to the efforts of man and society as they move towards the future. Therefore its main function is to build the society as per man's aspirations and to develop the kind of manpower that the society needs.

Education has many functions to perform, both to train procedures and to develop the individuals in society and also to strengthen and develop the society of which the individuals are integral parts. Therefore the functions of education comprises of two aspects:

A. *Functions of Education in the development of the individual*
B. *Role of Education in National Development*

A. Functions of Education in the development of the individual

Education is the complete development of the individuality of the child so that he can make an original contribution to human life according to the best of his capacity. - T P Nunn

Education is an investment in people. So education must take into consideration the manpower needs of the country, the relationship between education as an investment and its contribution to economic development. Human Resource Development is the major responsibility of education.

Individual Development is the stepping stone to Human Resource Development. *Individual development signifies the capacity to fulfill all one needs — safety, survival, self-esteem, recognition and self-actualisation.* It means the identification and development of ones capabilities to the fullest. Individual development enables development of a balanced integrated personality which helps one to lead a complete and harmonious life. So in order to achieve this, education has to perform a number of functions.

The Functions of Education in the development of the individual are focussed on the following aspects:

- Improved quality of individual
- Social participation
- Economic betterment
- Political contribution
- Achieving the harmonisation of the freedom and well-being of the individual with the strength and well-being of the society
- Catering to the individual need for continuing education by
  - — integration of Formal, Non-Formal and Informal modes of education
  - — teaching how to learn
  - — providing orientation in different areas with a variety of approaches
  - — providing specific education as a basis for qualification in technological careers

Having listed the aspects of the functions of education for the development of the individual, we proceed to explain each of these aspects.

(i) Improving the quality of individual

A nation's progress depends on the quality of individuals that form the society of the nation. Just as drops combine together to form the ocean, the individuals combine to form the society that forms the nation.

Education contributes to the development of the personality of the individual. Education enables the individual to realise his or her potential by providing opportunities to discover his talents and develop them, by giving full freedom for self-expression, creative thinking, critical awareness thereby enabling the individual to liberate himself or herself from all inhibitions and fears. Individualisation of education and diversification of courses caters to individual differences and provides opportunities for the individual to discover himself, make his own decisions and develop his special abilities. Education develops the skills of self-learning and thus provides permanent education. Education has to prepare the individual to face the challenges of life and of social transformation. ***Therefore, it provides counselling regarding choice of options and orientation in economic and occupational aspects of life.***

(ii) Creating Awareness

Creating awareness is essential to facilitate an individual to live a happy, prosperous life of fulfillment and self actualisation. The awareness created are the following types:

- **Health awareness** — to enable the individual to lead a healthy life free from disease.
- **Environment awareness** — to provide the individual with the means of benefiting from the stimulations of his environment, orienting the individual about the need for conserving natural resources, avoidance of pollution and remedying environmental degradation thereby enabling each individual to render his interactions with his environment more rich and structured within the limits imposed by any kind of social life.
- **Economic awareness** — to orient the individual in the economic and occupational aspects of life and develop in him the attitude to avoid wastage of resources and save resources and energy.

- **Social awareness** — to enable the individual to participate in social development by rising above personal interests, understand social problems and contribute towards tackling them.
- **Political awareness** — to enable the individual to become a good citizen and making him aware of his responsibilities and duties towards the family, society and nation and his rights according to the Indian Constitution for social justice and freedom. The individual has to be oriented about the legal provisions in the constitution that he can avail of, to fight against injustice and exploitation, as a citizen and as a consumer.
- **Consumer awareness** — to create awareness about that individuals as consumers can achieve an acceptable quality of life through a need-oriented process of development, making the individuals aware regarding their responsibilities, concern, solidarity and rights as a consumer.
- **Cultural Awareness** — to make the individual aware about his own culture as a part of the national culture. An individual must be made to rise above blind beliefs and traditions and develop a scientific rational attitude. Education has to enable the individual to enrich his leisure life with involvement in cultural activities thereby developing creativity.

(iii) Providing opportunities for vocational efficiency and continuing education

Knowledge explosion and developing trends in every field necessitates an individual to constantly reconstruct and restructure his experiences. Education has to motivate the individual to use memorised factual knowledge and form the keys to the use of communication and documentation media and to evolve working methods for recording, classifying, processing and interpreting information.

(iv) Development of Attitudes

Education has to prepare the individual for change. It has to enable the individual to learn to be himself. It has to help the individual to formulate his or her own value system and develop a strong character, positive thinking and positive attitude to life with a creative problem-solving approach. Education has to create a dynamic, non-conformist, non-conservative frame of mind.

Thus the functions of education in the development of an individual are:

i. Satisfaction of physical, mental and spiritual need and of those arising from continuous perception and awareness.

ii. Development of Personality — physical, mental, social and emotional through varied and enriching experiences to discover and develop talents.

iii. Character building through transmission of culture and inculcation of values.

iv. Providing vocational training and developing vocational skills for improving vocational efficiency of the individual through continuing education.

v. Education has to provide opportunities for —

- realisation of potentialities
- making correct choices
- economic betterment
- enriching leisure life

B. FUNCTION OF EDUCATION IN NATIONAL DEVELOPMENT

To provide educational opportunities for all is an essential need in all democracies; equally, to provide an education suited to differences in individual interests and abilities is a change demanded in the interests of justice and educational progress.

— I L Kandel

Before dealing with the functions of National Development it is essential to understand what National Development means and the dimensions of National Development.

What is National Development?

National Development means growth. expansion, reconstruction in economic, political, social and cultural dimensions.

The Human Development Reports (1991-93) have considered human development as the process of enabling people to have wider choices. Income is one of the choices but it is not the sum total of human life; health education, a good physical environment and freedom of action and expression are equally important. The Eighth Plan considers human development as the ultimate goal and gives priority to generation of adequate employment opportunities, building up people's institutions, controlling population growth, universalisation of elementary education, eradication of illiteracy, provision of safe drinking water and primary health facilities to all and growth and diversification of agriculture.

National Development must bring about appropriate development for all, specially the down trodden and the neglected. It should aim at development of India as a whole. It should be a process of institutional change. National Development should comprise of comprehensive and broad based programmes of sustainable development encompassing education, manpower planning and national, political and linguistic integration.

The characteristics of National Development are:

- It has a wide ranging scope of human activity that includes the attitudes of the people, the various scientific disciplines and introduction of many forms of expertise.
- It ensures a right place for India in the community of Nations.
- It derives largely from the power to develop and utilise the capabilities of its people.

DIMENSIONS OF NATIONAL DEVELOPMENT

The dimensions of National Development are mainly fourfold, namely, *Economic, Political, Social and Cultural,* and is presented in the following manner:

After discussing the concept of National Development and its dimensions, we now deal with the *functions of Education in National Development.*

Economic	***Political***	***Social***	***Cultural***
* Building a socialistic pattern of society	* Individual liberty of thought and speech	* Rising above caste system	* Basis of entire fabric of national progress
* Ensuring increased wages for all	* Freedom of association	* Respect for women	* Integration and solidarity
* Bridging the gap between the rich and the poor	* Due process of law and equality before law		* Signifies the implementation of the principles of unity in diversity
* Village and rural upliftment	* Right to vote		* Values ingrained - co-operation, co-existence, spirit of harmonious living
* Urban development	* Parliamentary democracy		* Way of life
* Ensuring full and proper employment for every individual			* Every individual - a significant link in the human chain
* development of agriculture			* Developing a global concern for Mankind as
* Provision of food and shelter			

The educational tasks of the nation are the bases for the tasks of education in National Development. The educational tasks of the nation are as follows:

- taking leadership in piloting and manning a future which will ensure better life to all.
- paying increased attention to —
- civic and political needs of the nation
- developing new attitudes towards government and law

- bringing about effective participation in the political process
- placing national interests and well-being above narrow level of local interests
- social and personal needs of the nation
- improving the health and well-being of the people
- solving the problems of physical and mental health as they arise
- maintaining the individual's self-respect and self-confidence to new surroundings
- relating the new cities with the rural communities in a spirit of partnership
- increasing the respect of different age groups for one another
- catering to the economic and technological needs of the nation.
- selecting and educating qualified individuals for high level positions.
- equipping technical and agricultural power with skills for maximum efficiency in utilising natural resources.
- developing a new spirit of economic innovation.
- building new attitudes towards saving, investing and purchasing.

Education plays a vital role in National Development. The functions of education for achieving National Development are:

i. *Manpower Planning* keeping in mind —
   - nation's needs
   - available resources
   - potential for contribution

ii. *Human Resource Development through training for citizenship, leadership, personality development and for developing vocational skills*
   - increasing productivity
   - improving quality of life

iii. *Participation in National progress*

iv. *Developing National Character*

- integrity, character building, values, work culture and commitment, emotional integration, nationhood and patriotism

v. *Modernisation and Social Change*

- cultural orientation
- rational outlook and scientific temper

Besides these, the important tasks to be achieved by education are as follows:

- transformation of the lives of the people by the processes of growth under free institutions.
- producing a surging interest and liveliness important for development.
- making people conscious (conscientising the people) of their problems, problematising and developing their attitudes, raising their aspirations, energising them to work for their own development.
- making possible economic democracy that raises social mobility.
- stimulating development by diplomatically convincing them that ***tomorrow need not be the same as yesterday. Change can take place.***

Having defined all the tasks before education for achieving National Development, it is necessary to understand the factors that hamper National Development. The following are the barriers to National Development:

- Large population
- Food problem
- Unemployment
- Communalism
- Regionalism
- Large, unlimited, political parties
- Multiplicity of languages
- Disparity in standards of living
- Regional imbalances
- Lack of good leaders

- Wars
- Natural calamities, floods, cyclones
- Unnatural calamities
- Financing of education
- Problems of standards in education

In order to achieve National Development by accomplishing the tasks, education has primarily to overcome the barriers to National Development by providing education with specific aims in the following manner.

1. Education for Personal and Social Development:

Personal development alone may make individuals self-centred. So personal development has to lead to social development. For example, an individual becoming a doctor or an engineer is a personal development. After acquiring the qualifications, if he works for the society he contributes to social development, otherwise it leads to brain-drain.

Unless there is a coordination between the expectations and aspirations of an individual and the society, conflicts and tensions will come in the way of achievement. Therefore *education for personal and social development* is essential.

The education for personal and social development will have to develop loyalty and responsibility in the individual to an ever-widening social group. In order to create a better environment, new attitude will have to be developed towards physical environment. *Scientific temper and individual and public health* can be achieved by enhanced science education and health education. It is necessary to *regulate man-made environment* with the help of the experiences of the past and futuristic approach, with the help of Social Science Education. *Character Formation* can be achieved through a well-planned value-oriented education. So education must produce young men and women of whom it can be proud.

2. Education for Social Change

Just as the river is constantly flowing, society is undergoing constant change. New ideas, new developments and changes in the culture require that society has to adapt to all these recurrent changes. It is always noticed that a dynamic society which changes according to the time progresses. A static society suggests a status-quo situation. Therefore, social change is an essential requisite for National Development. Education for change has to be planned on the basis of the following criteria:

- It must take into account prevailing beliefs and structure.
- It must be aware of the relationship of this structure to patterns of action, social institutions and goals. For example, the changes in the inter-relationship in the family and organisation have to be taken into account while planning education for social change.
- It cannot afford to ignore the magnetic force of city lights which will shape and condition the ways in which Formal Education is used or abused in the name of national development. For example, it is generally observed that over-urbanisation and migration to the cities due to the glamour of city life leads to white-collared crime and abuse of formal education.
- The future must be the guiding principle of general education.
- It must find meaning in the order, processes and goals of the culture for which it is intended. For example, the festivals and religious ceremonies must be viewed scientifically and their significance should be clearly understood.
- It must come to grips with the urgent problems of culture. For example, the emphasis given to the birth of sons alone and the evils of dowry system can be tackled by developing desirable attitudes among the student community.
- It must remain hospitable to continuous experimentation and reconstruction. Community development programmes can achieve this effectively by utilisation and mobilisation of community resources.
- It must focus on content. Special efforts should be made to include upto-date information with appropriate application and interpretation. For example, utilisation of alternate energy resources and conservation of energy resources can be included in the content of

education. Recently proposals have been made to incorporate information on AIDS and Sex education in the content of school education. However, the mode of incorporation and the weightage to be given will have to undergo changes according to the changes in the magnitude of the problem.

3. Education for Economic Growth

Economic development is the predecessor to National Development. The greatest barrier to national development is the economic backwardness and poverty, under-employment and unemployment. In order to overcome this barrier, Education for Economic Growth is essential. The *salient features* of education for economic growth are the following:

i. Integration of education and training

This can be done by providing on the job experiences and conducting workshops.

ii. Developing vocational skills and job-oriented training

In order to have highly skilled personnel in Industrial Organisations, it is necessary to develop vocational skills through vocationalisation of education and job-oriented training. Linkage should be established between industries and agriculture with education. This linkage will enable education to provide the right type of work-force for these organisations.

iii. Developing work-ethos

A healthy work-culture is essential for the progress of our nation. This can be developed by inculcating the value of industriousness and dignity of labour in students from the very begining. It is with this objective in view that *work experience* and later *socially useful productive work* have been introduced in the school curriculum.

iv. Human Resource Development for Increased Productivity

Human Resource Development is the nucleus for Man Power Planning. So self-sufficient and satisfied individuals will make a major contribution to the nation's productivity and progress.

v. **Achieving excellence through quality control**

The efficacy of productivity greatly depends on quality control. In trade and commerce, quality control is one of the basic factors of economic growth. So total quality control is the motto of successful industrial organisations. Hence it is important to achieve excellence through quality control. Education for economic growth has to instil the values of achieving excellence and maintaining standards.

vi. **Consumer Awareness**

Marketing techniques and Marketing Research and Development are important aspects that has to be included in the education for economic growth. Self-employment has been considered to be one of the strategies to tackle the problem of unemployment. So entrepreneurship training with emphasis on developing an attitude of industrial enterprise and their related skills is one of the vital aspects of education for economic growth.

4. Education for Social and Personal Integrity

Growth-oriented development of organisations is the core of national development. Growth-oriented development will have to be based on sound principles of values like integrity to find a prominent position in the commercial world market. Hence education has to play a dominant rôle in developing social and personal integrity by providing value-oriented education. The salient features of education for social and personal integrity are the following:

- rational outlook in judging the pros and cons of concepts, views and products
- scientific temper leading to scientific humanism
- inquiry training enabling individuals to establish relationships with a research attitude
- intellectual honesty in accepting and utilising other's contribution with proper accreditation
- value-orientation to inculcate the values of honesty and integrity.

5. Education for Civic and Political Freedom

Inspite of the fact that we are supposed to have established a democratic society, yet it is often found that the principles of civic sense and environmental awareness and many other essential qualities of democratic citizenship are lacking in our society. Besides this, we still find exploitation and social injustice rampant in various strata of society. The basic reason for this condition is lack of social and political awareness. Therefore Education for Civic and Political Freedom has to play a vital role in creating this awareness. The salient features of the programmes for education for civic and political freedom are the following:

i. Creating awareness regarding

- human rights and duties and provisions in the Indian Constitution
- law and justice
- social problems and responsibilities
- environment protection

ii. Developing

- critical awareness
- social skills
- skills of creative problem-solving
- effective decision-making
- attitude of commitment to the nation and to its welfare
- skills of transactional analysis. Transactional analysis enables one to analyse transactions and thereby improve relationships and effective communication.
- skills of stress management and managerial skills

6. Education for National Unity

National Unity is a basic essential attribute of a developing democracy. National Unity in other words signifies *National Integration*. The basic principles underlying Education for National Unity are orientation to the concepts of *unity in diversity* by inculcating the values of respect for cultural traditions and their contributions. A *spirit of nationhood* has to be developed by building national character. Through *international understanding* the ***global village perspective*** is created. For example, Olympics and Asian Games help in developing a global village perspective. These can be emulated by school-college complexes where the activities can be organised in a similar manner.

7. Education for All

Education for All is one of the major objectives of the National Policy on Education 1986. This aim has evolved with a view to achieving social and political participation in National Development. *The main thrust of education for all is to develop the capacity of the individuals to the fullest.* The measures that can be adopted to achieve this objective are as follows:

- total literacy
- functional literacy for participation in national development
- universalisation of elementary education
- synthesis of formal, non-formal and informal education
- distance education

Thus education must perform the task of a catalytic agent achieving sustainable development with a holistic approach using appropriate technology for empowerment of the people and social cohesion. It must spread economic opportunity and maximise equity. It must use methods of analysis and interpretation rather than rote-memorisation.

SUMMARY

I. **Functions of Education in the development of the individual**

i. Improving the quality of the individual

ii. Creating Awareness —

- Health awareness
- Environmental awareness
- Economic awareness
- Social awareness
- Political awareness
- Consumer awareness
- Cultural awareness

iii. Providing opportunities for vocational efficiency and continuing education

iv. Development of attitudes

Thus the functions of education in individual development are:

a. satisfaction of needs - physical, mental, spiritual and those arising from continuous perception and awareness

b. development of personality

c. character building

d. providing vocational training and improving vocational efficiency through continuing education

e. provide opportunities for -

- realisation of potentialities
- making correct choices
- economic betterment
- enriching leisure life

2. Functions of Education in National Development

i. Dimensions of National Development — economic, political, social and cultural

ii. Barriers to National Development

iii. Aims of education in National Development:

- Education for Personal and Social Development
- Education for Social Change
- Education for Economic Order
- Education for Social and Personal Integrity
- Education for Civic and Political Freedom
- Education for National Unity
- Education for All

4

GOALS OF EDUCATION

- *Importance of goals of education*
- *Determinants of goals of education*
- *Pre-Independence aims of education*
- *Post-Independence goals of education*

Every educational act is part of a process directed towards an end. These ends are dictated by general, ultimate aims which are essentially laid down by society. **— Edgar Faure**

Goal Setting: Rationale

Goal setting is an important process for achieving success in life. Any activity which is undertaken is directed towards the realisation of a goal. Goal setting gives direction to the activity, facilitates efficient objective-based planning and clarity in orientation of the functionaries implementing the activity. Programme Evaluation and Assessment of the performance of those involved in the implementation of the programme is made possible. Consequently this enables the maintenance of a high standard and achieving excellence by analysing the cost benefits.

Goals of Education: Importance

Education is a meaningful activity covering the entire span of an individual's life from birth to death. Therefore it has to be a well-planned, goal-oriented phased activity. Goals of Education, therefore perform mainly three functions, all of which are normative. Firstly, they give direction to the educative process. Secondly, they motivate. Thirdly, they induce the learner the energy necessary to accomplish them. They give direction to the process of education. They are need-based and related to life. They enable the planners to review the cost benefit and make education cost — effective. They facilitate monitoring and evaluation.

Determinants of Goals of Education

The sources of Goals of Education are the factors which enable one to determine the goals. They are as follows:

- Political Ideologies
- Social and economic problems
- Philosophical concepts and ideas
- Schools of educational thought

Political Ideologies

Political systems have influenced the goals of education. In ancient times when monarchy was the prevailing political system, the aims of education were determined by the policies of the ruling monarch. In Fascist nations, the aims of education were mainly to fulfill the needs of the state. Socialism emphasize equality of opportunities and development of the individual according to the need of the society. In a democracy, the aims of education emphasize maximum development of the potential of the individual, that is, chiefly based on Manpower Planning and Human Resource Development. Besides these, the goals of education are influenced by the priorities given by the government policies to the aspects of awareness regarding social and national problems like problems of poverty, population explosion and depletion of resources and public health.

Social and Economic Problems

While social and economic problems are mostly tackled by the government policies, yet social and economic problems as applicable to the development of individual and society form one of the major determinants of goals of education. Thus inculcation of social values like National Integration and Conservation of Resources and Cultural Heritage have an important place as goals of education.

Philosophical concepts and ideas

From ancient times character formation for leading a good virtuous life and self-realisation have been the major goals of education. Now with the changing concepts and modern philosophy the aims as given by the UNESCO Report, *Learning-to-be* are as follows:

- Scientific humanism, which means scientific thought and language, rules of objectivity and training of scientific minds.
- Creativity, based on the instincts of security and adventure, quest for new values, creative thought and action.
- Social commitment, which means political education, practice of democracy, participation, education in economics and international education.
- Complete man, namely - physical, intellectual, emotional and ethical integration of the individual into a complete man.

Schools of Educational Thought

The goals of education were influenced by the educational ideas of the exponents of the various schools of educational thought. The schools of educational thought are *Naturalism, Idealism, Realism, Pragmatism and Existentialism.* The goals of education according to these schools are as follows:

Schools of Thought	*Goals of Education*
1. Naturalism	Development of the individual according to his needs and interests.
2. Idealism	Character formation, Value inculcation Spiritual development
3. Realism	Producing man of world affairs, developing a complete man.
4. Pragmatism	Developing a fully functioning individual, Harmonious development.
5. Existentialism	Complete living, enrichment of mind, improvement of quality of life.

Individual vs Social Aim

Individual aim means *development of the individuality of human beings.* Individualism was emphasised by ancient educational thinkers and Greek philosophers. In the medieval times collective teaching was adopted and individual aim was not emphasised. Educationists like Roüsseau, Pestalozzi, Froebel and Nunn emphasised development of individuality as the main aim of education. The narrow meaning of individual aim of education is self-expression, all-round development of the child's abilities and natural development. The wider meaning is self-actualisation. The factors responsible for emphasis on individual aim of education are individual differences suggested by biological sciences and emphasised by modern psychology. According to the views of progressivists the progress of the world is due to the contribution of individual. To the spiritualists the good of the society lies in the infinite value of the individual person. The democratic ideals emphasise the freedom of the individual. All these influences combined together are known as the individual aims.

Social aim is opposed to individual aim as the basic principle of social aim is that man is a social animal and develops his personality in society. In the extreme form of socialism, the individual is subordinate to the state. Individuals have to sacrifice their own interests for the welfare of the state. This concept was held in ancient times in Sparta and other city states of Greece. The wider meaning of social aim is the democratic view of the social aim of education, which is to make individual socially efficient for a democratic society. *Social efficiency* means *economic efficiency.* Further, it includes *negative morality,* that is, readiness to sacrifice one's own interests to protect social interests, and *positive morality,* that is, willingness to sacrifice one's interests when they do not contribute in any way to social progress. Every individual must be educated to be interested in society. He must know what he owes to society. *School is a replica of society.* Social skills must be developed in the individual. The values of social heritage and human co-existence must be inculcated from the beginning.

The individual aim propagated by Rousseau, Pestalozzi, Herbart, Froebel, Rabindranath Tagore was criticised as impracticable. It was stated to be disregard to man's social nature thereby creating an environment leading to harmful consequences such as self-centredness, problems of adjustment and possibility of disintegration of society and isolation of the individual from society.

The social aim propagated by Bagley and Dewey were criticised as unpsychological as it suppressed individual freedom and hindered creativity and developed narrow nationalism.

Experts like Adams, Mac Iver and Nunn emphasise synthesis between Individual and Social Aim. *The principles of the synthesis are every individual is a component of society.* Man's gregarious instinct impels him to live in a society. Society affords protection to the individual. Human feelings are cultivated. *As Rusk states, "Individuality is of no value and personality is a meaningless term apart from social environment. Individual and social aim are complementary and can be pursued at the same time."*

Pre-Independence Aims of Education

In ancient India, the goals of education were influenced by the concept of Purusharthas or the goals of life, viz. Dharma, Artha, Kama, Moksha. Education was a means to prepare the individual to live a virtuous life as laid down by the scriptures. The four goals of life, the original concept, the present concept and the education for it are as follows:

1. Dharma

Original concept: Performance of religious rites and performance of one's duties efficiently according to the Bhagwad Gita.

Present concept: Adherence to duty to oneself, family, society and nation and achieving excellence.

Type of education

General education providing scope for all-round development

2. Artha

Original concept: Acquiring wealth by honest means

Present concept: Earning by a well-selected and satisfying vocation

Type of education

Vocational education will not only provide vocational training but also sow the seeds of work-culture.

3. Kama

Original concept: Fulfilment of erotic anaesthetic desires, refraining from mal practices.

Present concept: Satisfying one's desires for aesthetic experience and pleasure.

Type of education

Aesthetic education, that is, education in performing and visual arts and crafts.

4. Moksha

Original concept: Liberation from worldly bondage.

Present concept: Self actualisation

Type of education

Liberal education with a wide range of options.

General Aims

These general aims have been advocated by Indian and Western thinkers.

Character Formation

The importance of character formation as a goal of education was advocated by Plato, Aristotle, Herbert Spencer, Pestalozzi, Rousseau, Swami Vivekanand, Mahatma Gandhi and Swami Dayanand. Man's character is an invaluable asset. According to Emerson, *"Character is a reserve force and its power is felt even in the absence of any external means."* Character is universal wealth. It is the greatest of ornaments.

Character means whatever is engraved in the mind. It is reflected in the words and actions of an individual. Character is based on the principle *Knowledge is Virtue.* It comprises of social virtues like absence of boastfulness and deceit, non-violence, forbearance, steadfastness and self-control. The intellectual component comprises of intelligence, memory, intuition and reasoning power. Values like purity, truthfulness and non-stealing are the core-components of character.

Character formation is hampered by wrong examples set by parents and teachers, egoistic tendencies of children, lack of co-ordination between school and home and unsatisfied basic needs. The strategies for character formation are by providing value-oriented education directly through stories and anecdotes and indirectly through value-discussion method. The foundations of character formation are laid effectively in Home Education.

Cultural Aim

Conservation and transmission of culture builds up a cultured and refined man. Culture adds grace to human life. It helps in refining personality, making social adjustment, understanding and improving society and maintaining the continuity of cultural tradition. The inculcation of common culture and the principle of unity in diversity promotes national integration and love for our cultural heritage. This goal can be achieved by social studies and study tours to historical places.

Harmonious Development

Pestalozzi, Mahatma Gandhi and Rabindranath Tagore emphasised the importance of harmonious development as a goal of education. Harmonious Development connotes the following aspects:

Balanced personality development through integrated physical, mental, social and spiritual development.

Internal harmony through the development of a balanced integrated personality

External Harmony through healthy social inter-relationship and humanistic approach.

This goal can be achieved through varied rich experiences and education for peace.

Complete Living

This goal of education was advocated by Herbert Spencer. The underlying principles are the following:

- Every person should be able to keep himself in sound health and to satisfy his basic needs.
- Every person should be able to follow some vocation and to earn his living by honest means.
- Education necessary for continuation of the race must be given.
- He must know how to behave with others.

- He must be properly educated to spend his leisure time gainfully in whatever manner he likes.

In order to achieve this goal, the following aspects should constitute Education for Complete Living:

- Transactional Analysis to improve social inter-relations and communication.
- Meditation and Yoga for stress management.
- Time management for efficient organisation of work to enable one to find time for all that one desires to accomplish.

Thus the pre-independence goals of education and the general aims of education as commonly stated by Indian and Western philosophers emphasise the development of the individual's personality, inculcation of values and character formation to enable him to lead a good virtuous life with enlightenment and enrichment leading to self-realisation.

Post-Independence Goals of Education

The historical events and political situations bring about radical changes in social needs and social development. During the British rule, education in India on the whole, the cultural base and national objective of Indian Education had suffered a serious setback. After India became independent in August 1947, the need for radical change in the aims and structure of education was felt by the educationists, national leaders and social reformers. Establishing a democracy and nation-building necessitated social awakening and education for democratic citizenship. In the words of our late Prime Minister Pt. Jawaharlal Nehru, *"Great changes have taken place in the country and the educational system has to be in keeping with them. The entire basis of education must be revolutionised."*

In order to achieve the restructuring of education to cater to the needs of an independent India, various commissions were set up from time to time to review the situation and set the goals of education and formulate the curriculum accordingly.

Radhakrishnan University Education Commission (1948)

The first task was to review Higher Education as the youths are the major components of the society that is to be built. It was also important to understand the term 'democracy' and the characteristics of a democratic society. So the Radhakrishnan University Education Commission was appointed.

Dr. Radhakrishnan stated *"Democracy is a way of life and not mere political arrangement. It is based on the principle of equal freedom and equal rights for all its members regardless of race, religion, sex, occupation or economic status."*

The democratic aim of education was emphasised. The values of democratic aim as listed by the Commission were:

- Respect for dignity of the person
- Freedom — freedom of thought, expression, belief, faith, worship, vocation and movement. The democratic concept of freedom is rational freedom, i.e. freedom with self-restraint, responsibility, humane and just consideration of welfare of others.
- Equality of opportunity
- Group Living
- Faith in tolerance
- Faith in change
- Faith in peaceful methods

Therefore the goals of education according to the democratic aim were:

- multi-faceted development of the individual as an integral part of a democratic society
- community and social development
- worthy citizenship
- efficient leadership
- effective utilisation of leisure
- national integration and international understanding

AIMS OF SECONDARY EDUCATION COMMISSION

1. Development of Democratic Citizenship

The prime requisite of an effective democracy is efficient, capable, aware citizens who have love for the nation and are conscious of their social responsibilities. Education has to perform the task of preparing democratic citizens. According to the Commission, education can achieve this in the following manner:

(i) Clear thinking: In a democracy, there are many situations where major decisions have to be taken when one has to make his own choices. Therefore, education has to provide appropriate experiences to develop clear thinking in the students. Clear thinking means developing the capacity to differentiate truth from falsehood, facts from propaganda and keep away from fanaticism. Education has to enable an individual to collect facts, analyse them and interpret them with clarity. In the present context, this is fully applicable. For instance, when electing a candidate, one should be able to take into consideration all the aspects with a clear perception of both the positive and negative aspects. In everyday life, as consumers, various products are being advertised emphasising the plus points of each product. In order to decide which of the products are useful, economical and advantageous, clear thinking is essential. So, there is a great need to develop clarity of thinking among the students.

(ii) Clarity in speech and thought: Clarity in thinking to be useful has to be expressed and communicated effectively. Education has to develop clarity in speech and writing through effective teaching of languages. This will facilitate free discussion and peaceful exchange of ideas.

(iii) Art of living with the community: The value and skill of co-operation and harmonious coexistence have to be developed by inculcating the values of discipline, co-operation, social sensitivity and tolerance.

(iv) Developing sense of true patriotism and world citizenship: A sense of true patriotism has to be inculcated by developing interest in and appreciation for the social and cultural achievements of the nation, readiness to recognise the limitations and to work for educating them. Education has to develop the sense of world citizenship by making the students realise that they are not only citizens of their own country but world citizens.

2. Improving Vocational Efficiency

For a healthy democracy, citizens have to be self-sufficient and self-reliant and contribute to the economic development of the nation. Education has to achieve improvement of vocational efficiency by the following:

(i) Creating a new attitude to work

(ii) Developing dignity of labour,

(iii) Promotion of skill and efficiency by vocational training,

(iv) Introduction and implementation of SUPW (Socially Useful Productive Work) in schools to promote dignity of labour and create a work ethos.

Education has to provide avenues for vocational and technical training at all stages of education. Adoption of this measure will facilitate provision for efficient and skilled personnel. In the present context, improvement of vocational efficiency is one of the fundamental aspects of Human Resource Development.

3. Development of Personality

According to Secondary Education Commission, development of personality connotes enabling individuals to identify their own abilities and talents and develop them to the fullest capacity. Consequently, their sources of creative energy are released. This enables them to appreciate their cultural heritage. Education makes it possible to cultivate rich interests which they can pursue in their leisure time, thereby contributing to the development of their heritage.

Arts, craft, music. dancing and other hobbies have to be given due emphasis in curriculum designing. In the present context, we find that Human Resource Development emphasises Development of Personality to enable an individual to contribute in his fullest capacity to national development.

4. Development of the qualities of leadership

Effective leadership is the key to an effective democracy. This requisite of a developing democracy has been befittingly stressed by Secondary Education Commission. The Commission states that education must train students in discharging their duties efficiently in following others and leading the group. Education should identify those with leadership qualities and train them so that they are able to assume the responsibility of leadership in social, political, industrial and cultural fields or atleast in their own small groups.

In the present context, Panchayati Raj is greatly emphasised and leadership effectiveness is the indicator of a successful organisation. Education has to play a dominant role in the leadership training. Kamal Wadhwa, in his article on 'Charisma or hero worship in the supplement 'Ascent' of The Times of India, 13th March 1995 defines leadership in the following way. "*Leadership is the ability of a person to have a clear vision, out of which the leader sets the goals and objectives which can then form the basis of an organisation's paramaters. It is therefore a dynamic process of making people more effective, increasing their competence and through them achieving goals.*"

The above quotation substantiates the fact that effective leadership is of a paramount importance in every sector - governmental, public, private or corporate sector. Leadership training, today, is a major feature of workshops in Personality Development and Management.

The problems of National Development to be tackled by education were:

- Poverty and lack of financial resources
- Diverse religions and cultures and fundamentalism leading to communal disharmony
- Lack of awareness regarding rights and responsibilities

AIMS OF INDIAN EDUCATION COMMISSION (1964-1966)

Consequently the four aims of education stated by Indian Education Commission were as follows:

1. Increasing Productivity

The foundations of democracy were laid by the objectives given by Mudaliar Commission. The next step which had to be considered was the measures to make it an effective democracy. The prime factor that had to be considered was economic growth. So the first aim was increasing productivity to increase national income. The measures suggested for linking education with productivity were:

a. **Enhanced Science Education** by making science education an integral part of school education and even at university level.

b. **Introduction of Work Experience** in school curriculum — Work Experience means participation in productive work in the school, at home, in the workshop, factory or any work situation. This participation will develop a positive attitude to work and inculcate dignity of labour.

c. **Application of Science to Productive Work** - Every effort has to be made to link programmes to technology in every field of home management, industry, agriculture. This will enable to reduce drudgery and monotony of work. It will improve the working environment. For example, automation in offices, use of computers, etc.

d. **Vocationalisation** — Vocational skills should be developed through vocational courses and technical institutions. Emphasis has to be laid on establishing rural universities and technical institutions.

2. Achieving Social and National Integration

Social and national integration is the essential characteristic of a well-founded democratic society. Education plays an important part in building an integrated society. The measures suggested for achieving this objective are:

a. **Common School**: It is open to all children, irrespective of caste, creed, community, religion, economic conditions or social status. The opening of common schools will facilitate provision of quality education to all children.

b. **Social and National Services**: In order to bridge the gap between the educated and uneducated, rich and the poor and the urban and rural people, some form of social and national service has to be introduced as a requirement for the completion of courses. By the adoption of this measure, character building, discipline and dignity of manual labour can be inculcated.

c. **Promotion of National Consciousness**: This objective can be achieved by promotion of understanding and re-evaluation of our cultural heritage and an insight into the future.

3. Accelerating the Process of Modernisation

For a nation to be at par with developed countries, modernisation is a vital need. The process of modernisation involves curiosity and keen interest in new technological development. This is possible only if conservation is replaced by progressivism and traditionalism by rationalism. Education can achieve this by developing skills of independent study and the capacity to think and judge.

4 Cultivating Social, Moral and Spiritual Values

A national character can be built only if the people of the country have a strong value system. This value system is the outcome of national culture. The national culture evolves out of the synthesis of all the common aspects and values of all the cultures of different parts of the country. Therefore, education has an important role to play in cultivating social, moral and spiritual values.

Relevance to the present context

Considering the goals of education according to the Kothari Commission and their relevance to the present context, the following observations are made:

Increasing productivity through the enhancement of science education is very relevant considering the need to develop scientific temper and for economic growth leading to national development.

In order to build up an integrated society it is very essential to make provision for achieving national integration through education. The common school suggested in the report of Kothari Commission provides guidelines for the Navodaya Schools that are being established.

In the present electronic age it is very essential to develop positive attitude towards scientific and technological development. Besides use of appropriate technology is an important step towards urban and rural development. Hence, the goal of acceleration of modernisation is of great relevance in the modern context.

Last but not the least, various individual and social tensions and other influences are leading to different types of crimes and value-crisis. This necessitates a planned programme of Value Education. Hence the goal of education for moral and spiritual values is not only relevant but essential in the present context.

AIMS OF NATIONAL POLICY ON EDUCATION (1986)

The Secondary Education Commission (1952-54) and the Indian Education Commission(1964-66) had many recommendations keeping the progress of the nation in view. Inspite of the fact that efforts were being made to implement the recommendations, the hurdles in the way of reconstruction of education came in the way of implementation. As a result, the problems of education remained unsolved. Besides, developing trends necessitated a complete revamping of education. The main purpose of the National Education Policy was to tackle the problems of social and national development. Some of these are of such a great magnitude that they have to be tackled on a war-footing. Education has therefore to become a national movement with clearly defined goals. It has to be a system, planned efficiently with hindsight, insight and farsight. The recommendations of the earlier policies should be the starting point for deciding the priorities and setting the goals. The needs of the individual and society and national problems provide the insight and the farsight that enable educational planning for a better tomorrow.

The goals of education according to the National Policy on Education (1986) can be understood clearly if one establishes the relationship between the individual, social and national needs, the imminent problems demanding increased attention, the tasks to be fulfilled and the goals emerging from them.

(i) Education for all

One of the major national problem is the problem of illiteracy which hinders the plans for Human Resource Development. The task before the educationists was to provide facilities for education for all age groups irrespective of sex, caste or creed. So *the first goal of National Policy on Education was to provide Education for all.* This gave rise to further goals:

- to universalise elementary education
- to prevent the possibility of adult illiteracy in the years to come by reducing the rate of drop-outs in schools
- to accelerate Non-Formal Education and make education reach the remotest corners of the country.

(ii) Human Resource Development

The economic, social, cultural and technological progress of the nation had to be achieved. Therefore, the first step towards National Development is Human Resource Development. Developing Human Resources means building a learning society comprising of citizen, with a sense of responsibility and commitment to the nation besides being self-reliant, self-sufficient and achieving excellence in the field they belong to. So education has first to tackle the problem of population explosion and then concentrate on developing healthy efficient human resources. Therefore the goals of education are as follows:

- to create awareness in all citizens about the rapid rate of population growth.
- to create awareness about increasing levels of pollution and the hazards of environment.
- to develop a sense of responsibility and commitment among the individuals to the problems of the nation.
- to develop healthy individuals capable of contributing to the economic and social development.
- to make provisions for fulfilling the basic minimum needs and achieve the minimum level of learning at all stages.
- to develop social and vocational skills and provide a broad based skill-oriented vocational training that will equip the industries, agriculture and other professional organisations with a highly skilled work force.
- to establish linkage between Vocational and Professional Education and needs of industry, agriculture and commerce.
- to develop positive attitudes to work, co-operative activity and to life-long learning. A work culture has to be developed to have a dedicated committed work force.

(iii) Scientific and Technological Development

Scientific and technological developments are gaining access and being popularised and accepted in every field. Educational Technology and its effective use can help in making education more cost-effective by reaching the maximum number with minimum expenditure. The goals of education arising out of this need are:

- to strengthen both educational television (ETV) and audio programme capabilities and provide wider access to them.
- to improve science education in schools.
- to promote rural technology and appropriate technology to achieve economic development.
- to develop scientific temper.

- to acquaint students and teachers with the range of computer application and its potential as a learning medium.

(iv) Social and Cultural Development

An integrated cohesive society with a rich national culture and a national character is the distinctive character of a progressive nation. The national goals of socialism, secularism and preserving our cultural heritage have to be achieved. So the goals of education are:

- to create awareness regarding our cultural heritage
- to develop appreciation of the achievements of our national leaders
- to develop appreciation of diverse cultures of our country
- to promote values of national integration, secularism
- to remove barriers between the various age groups, diverse cultures, socio-economic groups and urban and rural community
- to provide equal opportunities to all communities for education
- to foster universal and eternal values oriented towards the integration of our people
- to achieve 'Unity in Diversity'
- to provide for development of Indian Languages
- to promote rational outlook

(v) Equalisation of Opportunities

National Policy on Education emphasises the goal of providing equal opportunity to the following sections of society.

- Equal opportunities were to be provided to scheduled caste, scheduled tribes, backward classes and minorities for education, job opportunity and economic progress.
- The handicapped were to be provided facilities for special institutions and where possible for integration into normal schools. The aim was to give them all the facilities to compensate for their handicaps and prove their abilities. For this the National Policy on Education

emphasised the development of attitudes in society to facilitate the integration of the handicapped.

- The National Policy on Education further laid emphasis on *the education and empowerment of women to* enable them to participate in the national activities. With this in view, the equality of sexes was *a major thrust on the National Policy on Education.*

Finally, the goals of education according to the National Policy on Education, 1986, are as follows:

- *Development of Human Resources*
- *Equity of Social Justice*
- *National Integration*
- *Protection of Environment*
- *Equality of sexes*
- *Observance of small family norm and improvement of quality of life*
- *Inculcation of Scientific Temper*
- *Removal of Social Barriers*
- *Equality of Educational Opportunity*

In order to achieve these goals, various strategies are adopted. These strategies are the salient features of National Policy on Education.

Thus the goals of education according to the National Policy on Education (1986) focussed on development of an achieving learning society through social transformation, modernisation and technology, cultural and social participation in national development.

Views of Ramamurti Committee on National Policy on Education (1986)

This committee was appointed in May 1990 and submitted its report on December 1990. The five principal concerns in the light of which the committee reviewed the implementation of the National Policy on Education were

(i) Equity and social justice

(ii) Decentralisation of educational management at all levels

(iii) Establishment of a participative educational order

(iv) Inculcation of values indispensable for creation of an enlightened humane society, and

(v) Empowerment of work.

The goals of education specified by the committee were:

- provision of a techno-informative knowledge base
- providing a climate for nurturing values - personal, social, cultural, national.
- providing opportunity for developing basic life skills, social skills and vocational skills
- empowering the students to play a catalytic role for promoting national cohesion and unity
- human resource development with emphasis on character development and transmission of values

Thus the goals of education are interwoven with the social, economic and political conditions of the times and the needs of the society.

SUMMARY

1. Goal setting gives direction to any activity that is undertaken.
2. Goals of education give direction to the process of education. They help us to review the cost benefit and make education cost effective.
3. Determinants of goals of education — political ideologies, social and economic problems, higher ideals of life, schools of thoughts, namely, Naturalism, Idealism, Realism,, Pragmatism, Existentialism.
4. Individual aim — development of the individual — Nunn, Rousseau, Pestalozzi and Froebel.

   Social aim — Individual has to sacrifice his own interests for the welfare of the state — Bagley and Dewey.

   Synthesis of individual and social aim suggested by Adams, MacIver, and Nunn.
5. General Aims: Pre-independence goals —

   1 Four Goals of life: Dharma — performance of duty, liberal education.

Artha	- earning by honest means,
	- vocational aim.
Kama	- satisfaction of erotic desires,
	- aesthetic education
	- cultural aim.
Moksha	- liberation,
	- value education.

- Character Formation
- Harmonious Development
- Complete Living

6. Post-independence goals of education —

Political situation	*Commission*	*Aims*
● Transition from co lonialism to independence	University Education Commission	Democratic aim of education
● Review of Second ary education, reconstruction of education, national awakening.	Secondary Education Commission (Mudaliar Commission 1952-54)	(i) Development of democratic citizenship. (ii) Improvement of vocational efficiency. (iii) Development of personality. (iv) Development of qualities of leadership
● Problems of devel oping a democratic society	Indian Education Commission Kothari (1964-66)	(i) Increasing productivity. (ii) Achieving social and national integration. (iii) Accelerating the process of modernisation. (iv) Cultivating social, moral and spiritual values.
● Implementation of reforms suggested by Kothari Commis sion, achievement of goals of constitution of India	National Policy on Education (1960)	(i) Social transformation (ii) Accelerated economic growth

Political situation	*Commission*	*Aims*
● Economic upliftment	Ishwarbhai Patel Committee (1977)	(i) Development of the capacity of self reliance (ii) Development of the value of cooperation & dignity of labour (iii) Development of the spirit of inquiry and initiative (iv) Economic & cultural development of the nation. (v) National Integration for realising the ideal of socialistic pattern of society.
● Imminent social and national problems	National Policy on Education (1986)	(i) Human Resource Development for National development. (ii) Equity and social justice. (iii) National Integration (iv) Environment protection, Conservation of resources. (v) Equality of sexes (vi) Observance of small family norm (vii) Improvement of quality of life.
● Review of National Policy (1986)	Ramamurthi Committee (1990)	(i) Provision of techno-information knowledge base (ii) Providing a climate for values (iii) Skill development (iv) Human Resource Development with emphasis on values.

5

CURRICULUM

- *Meaning of Curriculum*
- *Determinants of Curriculum*
- *Principles of Curriculum Construction*
- *Types of Curriculum*
- *Role of the centre, state, heads of institutions, teachers and parents in curriculum construction*

A house it has been said, cannot be properly built till all the materials for its construction - bricks, lumber and the like have been brought together in one place. Analogously, the student should not strive to solve social problems till he has stocked his mind with a wide assortment of curriculum materials. Curriculum material should be assembled not in general, but to realised and clearly defined end. — **Brubacher**

Curriculum is the core of an educational system. The interior decoration in general, and the artefacts that constitute it reflect the philosophy of life, and the personality of the designer to a great extent. Similarly, the subjects included in the curriculum in general and the units of the syllabi reflect the characteristic traits not only of the designer of the curriculum, but gives a global picture of the nation.

MEANING OF CURRICULUM

Etymologically, *curriculum means the ground which the pupils and the teacher cover to reach the goal.* Curriculum process is the transition from general aims to the particular objectives of the classroom. In curriculum planning, a three-step process is essential.

(i) *Ultimate goals* which are expected outcomes, are stated in terms of patterns or categories of behaviour.

(ii) *Mediate goals* which are patterns of expected behaviour at given stages over the educational period, are derived.

(iii) *Proximate goals*, i.e. specific objectives are set up.

The curriculum process consists of five phases:

1. Selection of aims, goals and objectives.
2. Selection of learning experiences to help attainment of the goals.
3. Selection of content (subject matter).
4. Organisation and integration of learning experiences.
5. Evaluation of the effectiveness of all phases.

Curriculum Development is a complex process involving many kinds of decisions and geared to the development of the individual and society.

Before dealing with some of the aspects of Curriculum Development, it is essential to understand the concept of curriculum.

DEFINITIONS OF CURRICULUM

"*Curriculum should be conceived as an epitome of the rounded whole of the knowledge and experience of the human race.*"

—Froebel

"*Curriculum is a tool in the hands of the artist (teacher) to mould his material (pupils) according to his ideals (aims and objectives) in his studio (school).*"

—Cunningham

"*Curriculum in its broadest sense, includes the complete school environment involving all the courses, activities, reading and associations furnished to the pupils in the school.*"

—Bent Rudyard and Kornenberg Henry

"*Curriculum includes all the learner's experiences in or outside that are included in a programme which has been devised to help him develop physically, emotionally, socially, spiritually and morally.*"

— Mudaliar Commission

"Curriculum is the total effort of the school to bring about desired outcomes in school and out of school situations."

— Sayler and Alexander

"Curriculum is a sequence of potential experiences set up in schools for the purpose of disciplining children and youths in group way of thinking and acting."

— B.O.Smith, Stanley and Shores

The characteristics of curricula are as follows:

- All curricula, no matter what their particular design, are composed of certain common elements.
- A curriculum contains statement of aims and\or specific objectives. It indicates some selection and organisation of content.
- It implies or manifests certain patterns of learning and teaching whether because the objectives demand them or because the content organisation requires them.
- It includes a program of evaluation of the outcomes.
- Curricula differ according to (i) the emphasis given to objectives, content, teaching-learning process, (ii) the manner in which the elements are related to one another, and (iii) the basis on which the decisions regarding each one of them are made.
- The decisions regarding the sequence of content and learning experiences vary according to the theories of learning applied.
- If learning is an organic whole, curriculum should not be piecemeal. If learning is developmental, the curriculum should embody a developmental sequence.
- A curriculum includes all the experiences a child has under the guidance of the school.
- It is the systematic arrangement of certain courses designed with certain objectives that are to be achieved.

Traditional Concept of Curriculum

The traditional concept of curriculum has been prevalent in our schools since a long time. The main objective of the educational programme was mastery over certain types of knowledge and skills. The teacher's attention was focussed on making the students learn the subjects of study according to a fixed syllabi, in a rigid set-pattern to enable to pass certain examinations. The pupil was given knowledge and skills which would make him become a mature and successful adult, according to the criteria of adults. He was prepared for a future as foreseen by his parents and teachers. The present needs of the child or as a youth later were not considered.

Modern Concept of Curriculum

According to this concept, education is a process intended to help the pupil to live in the present world and adapt himself to it according to his age and ability. Besides, he is encouraged to prepare for the future and also helped to build the future world in which his generation would live.

The modern concept of curriculum was clearly explained in the Report of Kothari Commission as follows:

"*The curriculum includes the sum total of experiences that a pupil receives through manifold activities that exist in the school — in the classroom, library, laboratory, workshop, playground and in the innumerable contacts between teachers and pupils. In this sense, the whole life of the school becomes the curriculum which can touch the life of the student at points and help in the evolution of balanced personality.*"

The fundamental characteristics of the new concept of curriculum are as follows:

- Textbooks and subject matter are not fixed rigidly and adhered to.
- Environment also provides learning experiences for him.
- The present needs of the pupil are emphasised and the school provides the material suited to cater to these needs and to bring about his intellectual, social and cultural development.
- A variety of experiences are provided to develop the personality of the child.
- Provision is made for the varying interests and abilities of the pupils.
- The principle of variety operates not only at the individual level but also at the institutional and state level. The criterion for this variety is the institutional and regional needs.

DETERMINANTS OF CURRICULUM

The development of curriculum comprises of the major tasks of formulating the objectives, selecting the content and deciding the focal points. The factors which guide the decision are the sources or the determinants of the curriculum. *In the words of Hilda Taba "Scientific curriculum development needs to draw upon analyses of society and culture, studies of the learner and the learning process and analyses of the nature of knowledge, in order to determine the purposes of the school and the nature of its curriculum".*

The sources of criteria for determining the main objectives of education, selecting the content and deciding the priorities are as follows:

- Analysis of culture and society
- study of the individual and his needs
- the learner and the process of learning
- nature of knowledge and the contribution of disciplines to mental, social and emotional development
- choice of values and philosophies

On the basis of these broad-based sources of criteria, the determinants of curriculum may be classified into three categories:

- Philosophical
- Psychological
- Sociological

Philosophical Determinants

The philosophical determinants are based upon fundamental principles of Educational Philosophy, national objectives, and schools of educational thought.

Goals of Education

The selection of content is decided on the basis of what is to be achieved and the goal to be reached. For example, the development of the individual is achieved with the help of a broad-based and skill-oriented activities. The goal of economic development is achieved with the help of measures to increase productivity.

National Objectives

The goal of national objectives arises out of the targets to be achieved in the path of progress towards national development. They are problem-oriented and focus on the problems that come in the way of development plans and their fulfilment, for example, population explosion and the resultant environment degradation. Therefore *creation of awareness* is the goal to be achieved.

Schools of Educational Thought

The schools of educational thought influence the formulation of objectives and selection of the content of the curriculum. The relationship between the school of educational thought, the goal of education and the content of the curriculum is made clear by the three-dimensional chart presented here under:

Psychological determinants

In child-centred education, and according to the modern concept of curriculum, the psychological factors play a dominant

School of Thought	*Principle*	*Curriculum Content*
Naturalism	emphasis on natural inclination	sciences which deal with nature
Pragmatism	utility, child's interests, experiences	liberal education, physical education, health education, environmental education,
Idealism	transmission of values, ideals, character formation inculcation of work culture	art education art, poetry, mental disciplines, social studies, SUPW, vocational training
Existentialism	development of human beings, leading a good life, development of complete man	study of humanities, moral and religious education, art, literature

Realism	practical utility, vocational efficiency, improvement of health, total development	science subjects, vocational education, health education, mathematics, economics, political science, geography, history

role in determining the curriculum.

Firstly, the study of the learner is necessary. His abilities, capacities, his interests, that is, the aspect of individual differences is an important determinant of the curriculum.

The stages of physical and mental development are an important factor not only in deciding what is to be included but also in deciding the units and the level to which they are to be taught. In other words, it helps the gradation of the content and selection of the activities, in accordance with the level to which it is to be taught.

The process of learning, the factors that promote learning provide guidelines for the curriculum construction to plan the teaching-learning strategies. The theory of motivation, the theory of personality development are the bases of selection of content.

The appropriate application of psychological theories to the process of curriculum construction enhances the utility and effectiveness of the process. By making the entire curriculum interesting, it makes it effective.

Sociological Determinants

A study of society is a pre-requisite of curriculum construction.

National Development is the sum total of economic, social, and cultural development. In order to achieve national development, learning society has to be built by providing the right type of education. So the curriculum has to be constructed keeping in mind the following factors:

- structure of society
- family patterns
- social needs
- social problems
- economic growth

The structure of society is constantly changing, according to changes from time to time. The changes have to be analysed. The curriculum has to be framed to cater to the changing social needs and aspirations. The material and human resources in society have to be explored and gainfully utilised for economic growth. Social awareness has to be created to develop a sense of commitment and involvement in tackling social problems. Activities that will develop social skills have to be included. Experiences of community living and group activities have to form a part of the curriculum. These experiences will promote social values of co-operation, team spirit and will help in developing social skills.

Political Determinants

The curriculum has to develop democratic values of social justice, equity, and secularism through social studies. Civics creates awareness regarding rights and duties according to law as a citizen, and rights and duties as a consumer too.

Thus, it may be stated that the determinants of the curriculum provide a blue print for constructing the curriculum and achieving the goals of education.

PRINCIPLES OF CURRICULUM CONSTRUCTION

On the basis of the various theories that determine the curriculum, principles of curriculum construction have been evolved. The principles of curriculum construction are of two categories: (i) general principles evolving out of the theories of educational thinkers and the review of commissions, and (ii) principles evolving out of the analysis of the tasks pertaining to curriculum construction.

The *principles of curriculum construction* emphasised by *John Dewey* were:

(a) **Principle of utility:** According to this principle the subjects included in the curriculum should be useful in solving problems and facing situations in life. For instance, the inclusion of consumer guidance and health and hygiene in the secondary school curriculum is essential from the utility point of view.

These subjects enable the individual to avail of his rights as a consumer, make the right choices and get the standard quality of service at right price. Health and hygiene enables the individual to solve his health problems and lead a healthy life.

(b) **Principle of Flexibility**: The curriculum should be flexible and not pre-determined and rigid. For instance, if a teacher finds that the class is losing interest either in the particular subject or particular topic, the teacher must be able to deviate from the set pattern. The curriculum must be capable of accommodating the changes in the child's interests and inclinations. It must be in accordance with the social requirements. The curriculum at the elementary stage must be based on the four-fold needs and interests of the child, viz. (i) Conservation and communication (ii) Enquiry and curiosity (iii) Construction, and (iv) Artistic expression.

(c) **Principle of child-centredness**: Child is the focus of education. The selection of content has to be in keeping with the child's interests and abilities. For example, the learning experiences provided at the pre-primary level should emphasise socialisation of the child rather than an ability to read and write.

(d) **Principle of life-centredness**: The subjects and activities included in the curriculum should be related to life. They should enable an individual to function efficiently and face the challenges in life. For example, bank transactions can be integrated with the teaching of simple interest in mathematics.

(e) **Principle of community-centredness**: Education has a dominant role to play in community development. The needs of the community and its problems should be the focus of selection of curriculum content. For example, the curriculum which is community centred is problem-oriented, and inculcates the values of co-operative action to tackle the problem.

(f) **Principle of correlation**: The elements of the curriculum cannot be isolated from one another. They should be viewed as an integrated whole bringing about the development of the child.

(g) **Principle of activity-centredness**: Learning through purposeful activity and actual life experiences makes the learning process interesting and enjoyable. The pupils are actively engaged in the process of learning.

Curriculum reconstruction in India was mainly according to the guidelines provided by the Secondary Education Commission (1952-54), the Kothari Commission (1964-66) and the National Policy on Education (1986). It is therefore interesting to study the Principles of Curriculum Construction stated by them.

The *principles highlighted by the Secondary Education Commission* were:

(h) **Principle of totality of experience**: This principle emphasises that the curriculum includes all the experiences that achieve the physical, mental, social and emotional development of the child.

(i) **Principle of variety and elasticity**: This principle signifies that the subjects included and the learning experiences should be varied according to the diversity of interests, the levels of intellectual development and the various talents and aptitude. Elasticity means the flexibility according to various stages and changing interests and changing social conditions.

(j) **Principle of core subjects**: This principle of including some common subjects like Languages, Science and Social Studies for all is emphasised by all the commissions. According to the National Policy on Education (1986) the national curriculum framework contains a common core along with other components that are flexible. The common core content includes history of India's freedom movement, the constitutional obligations and those essential for nurturing national identity.

(k) **Principle of linking with community life**: This principle is an extension of the Principle of Community-centredness stated by John Dewey. Besides basing education on the community need, this principle suggests involvement in community life and interaction with the community. For example. social service, especially the school camps provide opportunities for the students to live with the community, observe their way of life, understand their culture and their problems analytically and critically. Thus the principle of linking with the community promotes development of social values in the pupils, develops their problem-solving ability and their spirit of inquiry.

(l) **Principle for the use of leisure**: The Secondary Education Commission emphasises this principle and advocates education for leisure. The use of leisure in an appropriate manner develops creativity, aesthetic sense and may enable an individual to increase his income with the help of vocational skills.

(m) **Principle of inter-relation of subjects**: The inter-relation of subject means correlation of subjects and suggests an inter-disciplinary approach.

(n) **Principle of Need-based activity**: The Kothari Commission emphasises this principle as education has to cater to the needs of society and provide the man-power for social and economic development.

(o) **Principle of value-orientedness**: Both the Kothari Commission and the National Policy on Education (1986) emphasised the inculcation of values like social justice, equality of opportunity, equality of sexes, social values and democratic values.

(p) **Conservative Principle**: Conservation of cultural heritage, monuments, natural resources and wild life should be inculcated in the pupils from the very beginning through appropriately selected units in the syllabus of various subjects and organisation of appropriate co-curricular activities like field trips, visits, excursions, stamp collection, collection of pictures, etc.

(q) **Principle of creative training**: Education can be an enjoyable activity only if the curriculum stimulates and develops the creative abilities of the pupils. As Raymont rightly puts it, in a curriculum that is suited to the needs of today and of the future, there must be a definite bias towards creative subjects.

(r) **Principle of harmony:** Formal and informal education general, liberal and vocational education, individual and social aims should be skillfully interwoven into a harmonious whole paving the way for individual development and social upliftment.

The *principles of curriculum construction evolving out of the tasks involved in curriculum construction are discussed by Hilda Taba* in the following manner:

1. Principle guiding the formulation of objectives:

- clarity and specificity, i.e. breaking down complex behaviour into their components
- clear specification of expected behaviour
- clear distinction among learning experiences required to attain different behaviours
- objectives are developmental rather than terminal points
- objectives must be realistic and should include only what can be translated into curriculum and classroom experience

- scope of objectives should be broad enough to encompass all types of outcomes for which the school is responsible

2. Principles governing the selection of content

- validity and significance to the extent that it reflects the contemporary scientific knowledge and how fundamental it is (depth, breadth of application)
- consistency with social realities (capacity to transfer knowledge to situations)
- restoring and maintaining balance between intellectual proficiency and intelligent social perspective
- balance of breadth and depth (accumulation of knowledge, understanding fully basic concept as well as their application)
- selection of wide range of ideas to see which have application
- provision for wide range of objectives
- learnability and adaptability to experience of students
- appropriateness to the needs and interests of students (catering to individual differences)

3. Principles of organisation of the content

- establishing sequence (simple to complex, based on prerequisite learning, from whole to parts)
- providing for cumulative learning (step by step experience leading to more complex forms of argumentation, criticism and analysis of ideas)
- providing for integration
- unifying the curriculum (principle of correlation)
- combining logical and psychological requirement
- determining the focus
- providing variety of modes in learning

Thus we find both the treatments of principles of curriculum construction, viz., general and based on the various tasks involved have enunciated common principles, though the perspectives are slightly different.

TYPES OF CURRICULUM

According to the current patterns of organisation of curriculum, there are different types of curriculum. They are as follows:

i. Subject-centred or knowledge-centred
ii. Activity-centred or experience curriculum
iii. Undifferentiated curriculum
iv. Basic education curriculum
v. Life-centred curriculum

Subject-Centred Curriculum

Knowledge is divided in terms of isolated subjects. The sequence followed is the logical sequence pertaining to the particular discipline. The logic is determined by the subject specialist. Attaining mastery over the subject matter is the central task. The whole teaching-learning process is subject-centred and teacher-centred. This type of curriculum prepares the student for higher education but not for life.

According to some educationists, some subjects have value as mental discipline. Compartmentalised knowledge produces disciplined knowledge. It can be planned more easily and taught according to a fixed schedule.

The *criticisms* against the subject-centred curriculum are as follows:

- It does not facilitate individual development, independent thinking, creativity and active learning.
- It does not inspire the learner as excessive concern is for covering the portion.
- Subject-centred curriculum fosters mental passivity and fails to encourage active use of the knowledge that is acquired.
- There is insufficient experimentation in different ways of organisation of subject matter.
- Each subject becomes a dead end track and subjects are polished off at the end of the course. In other words, closing the book means closing the subject matter.

The fact that the subject-centred curriculum did not contribute to the individual's life is illustrated in the off quoted passage from *Whitehead*.

"There is only one subject matter for education and that is Life in all its manifestations. Instead of this single unity, we offer children Algebra from which nothing follows, Science from which nothing follows, History from which nothing follows, a couple of languages never mastered and lastly, most dreary of all, Literature, represented by plays of Shakespeare with philological notes and short analyses of plot and character, to be in substance committed to memory. Can such a list be said to represent life as it is known in the midst of the living of it? The best that can be said of it is that it is a rapid table of contents which a deity might run over in his mind while he is thinking of creating a world, and had not yet determined how to put it together."

Activity-Centred or Experience Curriculum

It is an attempt to counteract the limitations of the subject-centred curriculum especially passivity of learning and isolation from the needs and interests of children. The rationale of this approach comprises of the following facts:

- People learn from experience.
- Only that learning which is related to active purposes and rooted in experience translates itself into behaviour changes.
- Children are interested in learning those things that help them in fulfilling their needs.
- Learning is an active transaction. It involves learning to think logically, engaging in activities which are vital to him to achieve his personal goals and fulfil his needs.

The characteristics of activity curriculum are the following:

The activity curriculum is based on the following views:

Comenius — Whatever has to be learnt has to be learnt by doing.

Rousseau — Instead of making the child stick to his books, keep him busy with the workshop where his hands will work to the profit of his mind.

Dewey — Activity curriculum is a continuous stream of child's activities, unbroken by systematic subjects and springing from the interests and personality-felt needs of the child.

The *nature of activities* included are the following:

- All activities of head, heart and hand are included.
- The types of activities comprise of physical activities — physical training, games and athletics, action songs, hygiene, rest and meals.
- Environment activities — civics, history, geography, nature study, excursion, visits.
- Constructive activities — handwork activities pertaining to general science, constructive crafts.
- Imaginative activities — literature, dramas, stories, imaginative arts and crafts.
- Community activities — projects of different community works, self-government, social-service organisations.

All these activities must include those activities which help in the development of the individual.

Advantages of Activity-Centred Curriculum:

i. The Activity-Centred curriculum helps in sublimation of instincts especially the instincts of

a. curiosity and construction,

b. physical, intellectual and social development.

ii. It makes the process of education interesting and motivates the pupils for learning.

iii. It keeps the teacher alert and active.

Limitations of Activity-Centred Curriculum

- All education cannot be imparted through activity-centred curriculum.
- Overactivity may lead to lop-sided development.
- All the activities may not suit all the students. So, thought should be given to individual differences when planning the activities.

Experience Curriculum

Experience Curriculum is related to Activity Curriculum. Experience is the outcome of purposeful activity.

Experience Curriculum facilitates the process of learning, helps in social development and understanding environment. Experience may be direct or indirect. Direct experiences are those which provide first hand knowledge. These experiences are in the form of excursions, doing manual work, projects and craft work. The knowledge gained from these experiences is concrete. Indirect experiences are those which are given through text book, media, library services and educational films.

Undifferentiated Curriculum

Undifferentiated Curriculum is that curriculum which does not lead to any specialisation. It contains the minimum which has to become a part of every child's experience. It is fused curriculum. It is regarded as correlated or integrated curriculum.

Core Curriculum

Core Curriculum is a concept rather than an administrative arrangement. The concepts which are to be incorporated in the teaching-learning situation form the essence of the core curriculum.

The basis of the pattern of core curriculum are the key aspects of the rationale underlying the core theory.

(i) John Dewey's philosophy of experimentalism

(ii) Focus of learning upon fundamental human activities

(iii) Learning viewed as continuous reconstruction of experiences

(iv) Emphasis on problem-solving as an important part of learning

(v) Basic democratic values and the cultural factors emerging out of the dynamic changes in the western world

(vi) Acceptance of cognitive theories of learning — recognition of the role of cognition in human learning. It further recognised learning as a dynamic organic process. Learning includes not only verbal and motor responses but also attitudes and affective responses. In core programmes the emphasis is on objectives, problem-solving and reflective thinking.

The *salient features* of the core curriculum are as follows:

- It is general education aspect of teaching irrespective of social status or vocational choice.

- It is problem-oriented. The aim is to focus on the common problems of the learners.
- The process of learning is important as it is planned with a view to providing first-hand experiences to the learner. The emphasis is on total growth of the pupil - physically, mentally, socially, emotionally, spiritually.
- Core pattern is flexible providing for utilisation of learners ideas.
- A block of time, i.e. two or three periods at a stretch is necessary to facilitate proper functioning according to core pattern. Multi-media approaches are useful in making it effective.
- Guidance and counselling is an integral part of core curriculum.

Basic Education Curriculum

It was a system of education evolved as an education for living through life. The *main features* of the Basic Education Curriculum were:

- Education for life through participation in socially useful and creative work.
- Basic Education is imparted and developed round basic crafts.
- All subjects were correlated with craft.
- It was an activity curriculum based on *the principle of Learning by Doing* advocated by Pestalozzi, Froebel, Montessori. In this curriculum, pupil makes and creates something while learning. In Basic Education, activity is not mere play but productive work.
- Children should earn through the productive craft and provide finance for the school. Thus, the principle of self-sufficiency was to be achieved.
- Mother tongue was to be the medium of instruction.
- A link was to be established between education in the school and outside by involving the parents and community in the social and cultural programmes of the school.
- Basic education curriculum is a life centred curriculum.

Limitations of the existing curriculum and suggestions for improvement:

- The existing curriculum is still information-oriented and less skill-oriented.
- It lacks the capacity to develop the personality of the child and to develop the skills for facing the challenges of the world of work and situations in life.
- It does not develop insight into the mathematical and scientific concepts. Hence the capacity to apply these concepts is lacking. The pupils merely learn the concepts by memorisation.
- The variety of practical experiences acquired through experimentation is absent. Enjoyable and interesting activities are not included as part of the curriculum. As a result, the natural instincts of the child to explore and discover are not satisfied. So the child is bored by the routine of school life. There is hardly any scope for freedom of expression.
- The topics included in the syllabus are not relevant to life and sometimes give out-dated information.
- The curriculum does not develop the skill of self-study. After completion of the courses, the pupils are not in a position to satisfy the man-power requirements of the industries as they do not develop the job-oriented skills required for efficiency in their jobs.

The **measures that may be adopted for improvement** of the curriculum are:

- Emphasis on interpretation rather than the quantity of information.
- Creation of awareness and learning environment through true to life experiences.
- Simulation of conditions, visits to work places, surveys of families, group discussions, role play and skits or street plays to create awareness of social problems.
- Development of self-expression through co-curricular activities and aesthetic education.
- Vocationalisation of Education and nurturing of job-oriented skills.

- Objective-oriented synthesis of class room and out-of-school activities to enable the pupil to develop the personality, with a holistic approach to improving the quality of life.
- Synchronising class-room teaching with media programmes, newspaper and current issues.

ROLES OF THE CENTRE, STATE, HEADS OF INSTITUTIONS, TEACHERS AND PARENTS IN CURRICULUM CONSTRUCTION

Curriculum Construction in the initial stages, and later curriculum change is a co-operative activity. The centre plays an important role in co-ordinating, planning and other administrative aspects of curriculum construction. The state organises and conducts various activities at the state level. The heads of institutions are the key persons to create the congenial environment for experimentation, orientation and successful implementation. The teachers are the implementors of the curriculum. In fact, they have the capacity to weigh the pros and cons of the changes introduced and decide the '*to be*' or '*not to be*' of the planned changes. The parents represent an important section of society. They are, to a great extent, conscious of the targets they want their children to achieve. As members of society, they know what type of human resources the society needs. They are actively engaged in helping their children in their studies and are constantly endeavouring to tackle the problems encountered by the children. The pupils themselves, are in the process of learning the subjects, so they have first-hand experiences, though of course, there is ample scope for subjectivity and prejudices. Therefore, it is worthwhile considering the role of each of these factors in curriculum.

Role of Central Government

As far as education is concerned, the organisations which perform the functions of educational reconstruction are Ministry of Human Resource Development, National Council of Educational Research and Training (NCERT) and Central Board of Secondary Education (CBSE). Their functions are as following:

- Educational planning
- Orientation Courses for teachers
- Financing workshops and researches at all India level

- Co-ordination of researches conducted at State level
- Dissemination of the findings to the institutions concerned
- Follow-up work

Role of the State

- Implementation of the directives from Central Government
- Orientation of teachers at Regional level
- Conducting workshops on Text book writing
- Conducting research studies to try-out the changes
- Disseminating the research findings to the Centre

Heads of Institutions

- Studying the existing curriculum
- Orientation of teachers for implementation of the revised curriculum
- Motivation of the teachers to participate in curriculum research
- Providing the facilities for conducting researches and for innovative practices at institutional level and individual level
- Getting the researches processed and conveying the findings to the curriculum planners

Teachers

The teachers are the main implementors of the changes introduced in the curriculum. It is very essential that they have a complete understanding of the significance of the changes introduced. Besides it is most essential that they have a positive attitude to change.

- They should not think that the curriculum laid down should be blindly implemented. They should analyse the curriculum critically.
- They should be actively involved and participate wholeheartedly in the evaluation of the curriculum with an open mind and a research outlook.
- They should conduct action research and diagnostic studies to find out the problems of the children.

- They should be able to sift the genuine problems from those arising out of prejudices and biases.

Parents

Involvement of the parents in curriculum construction and getting their opinions will achieve two major purposes:

- They will be motivated to understand the changes introduced with greater interest and a rational outlook.
- Among the parents, there may be some subject experts who can make a great contribution towards the development of the subject and the accuracy of the information given.
- Besides, the parents' attitudes to a particular subject and to the children's understanding of the subject is vital in forming the children's attitude. For example, a single negative remark made by the parent is bound to prejudice the mind of the child.
- Parents are deeply involved in assisting their children in their studies. So they are capable of suggesting changes in the syllabus according to the difficulties encountered by them when teaching the units.
- Parents, who are in the industrial sector and are professionals in various fields are in a position to state what improvements can be made in the curriculum to provide efficient skilled work force for the industries and other work places.

Finally, it may be stated that Curriculum can become an effective tool in the hands of the teacher, if it evolves out of the cumulative ideas and experiences of the curriculum planner, heads of institutions, teachers, parents and last but not the least, the reactions of the students, who are deeply engaged in the process of learning. A co-operative activity, co-ordinated action and team-work are the pre-requisites of a good curriculum.

SUMMARY

1. **Meaning of curriculum** — definitions, characteristics, traditional and modern concept of curriculum.
2. **Determinants of Curriculum** — Philosophical, psychological, sociological and political determinants.

3. **Principles of Curriculum Construction —** emphasised by John Dewey, various commissions and Hilda Taba.
4. **Types of Curriculum** — Subject-centred or knowledge-centred, Activity-Centred or Experience Curriculum, Undifferentiated Curriculum, Core Curriculum, Basic Education Curriculum.
5. Limitation of the existing curriculum and suggestions for improvement.
6. Roles of the centre, state, heads of institutions, teachers and parents in curriculum construction.

6

CONTRIBUTIONS OF EDUCATIONAL THINKERS

"Education merely fleshes out the philosophical skeleton. It illustrates philosophic principles. Philosophical categories shed light on educational problems. Philosophy enters education when disagreements occur in policy, ambiguities arise in terms used or practice proceed or unexamined assumptions."

Brubacher

The concept of education and the various areas of education have been influenced by a number of factors but the nucleus of the principles of education is the off-spring of the educational thinkers. Educational ideas are not random opinions but are evolved out of the rich repertoire of experiences of the educational philosophers. Hence the biographical background, i.e. aspects of the biography have to be inter-linked with the philosophy and educational ideas leading to the contributions to education.

SWAMI VIVEKANANDA (1863-1902)

BIOGRAPHICAL SKETCH

Family Background

Narendra Nath as he was originally called was born in a Kshatriya family of Calcutta. His father was a lawyer and an attorney in the Calcutta High Court and provided the best education for his son.

Academic Background

A brilliant student that Narendra Nath was, he had excellent command over Sanskrit, Bengali and English. He was an orator. He was deeply interested in poetry, philosophy and comparative religion of East and West. He graduated from Calcutta University and was a classroom teacher for some time.

Narendra Nath transforms into Swami Vivekanand

Though religious, he was dissatisfied with the religious system in India and his search for God and quest for truth led him to Sri Ramkrishna Paramahamsa an Upanishadic seer, and an embodiment of Vedanta. Narendra's life was transformed and his aspiration for God-realisation was intensified. He fled from home, broke all ties became a sanyasi and travelled all over India preaching the Vedantic philosophy.

First messenger of India to cross the Atlantic and spread the Message of Vedanta

Swami Vivekananda was invited to speak and deliver the message of peace and harmony to the Parliament of Religions held at the World's Fair in Chicago in 1893. Through his soul - stirring lecture he unfolded the highest philosophical ideals in Vedanta to the congregation of world religious thinkers.

Mission of disseminating the message of Vedanta far and wide continued

After the congress, he was invited to lecture on Vedanta in almost all the largest cities of America and Harvard University. He was invited in 1896 to England to lecture at Oxford University where he met Prof. Max Muller. He addressed many meetings and spread the message of Vedanta. On his return, he was given an overwhelming reception.

A humble, dedicated devoted Sanyasi Swami - Vivekananda travelled throughout India preaching Vedanta:

Swami Vivekananda was invited by Rajas and wealthy people to lecture in various parts of India. Like an ordinary Sanyasi in rags and with a begging bowl he wandered all over India.

Established ashrams and started Ramkrishna Mission

During 1897 when famine and plague swept various parts of India, Swami Vivekananda established relief camps in different places. He started Ramkrishna Mission. Belur Math was established in 1899. Orphanages were started.

Founded Vedanta Society of San Francisco

In 1899 he was invited to California. Many scholars became his disciples. He founded the Vedanta Society of San Francisco.

Return to India

After his return he continued his mission with zeal . But his health started failing and he died in 1902 at the young age of 39 years.

PHILOSOPHICAL IDEAS

1. Vedanta is perfectly impersonal. It is eternal. The schools of Vedanta are not absolute systems but stages for helping the individual to proceed progressively towards the realisation of higher ideals.
2. God is impersonal and omnipresent. Man is incarnation of God.
3. The only God to worship is the human soul in the human body. Vivekananda preaches Vedanta as eternal communion of man with God.
4. All religions lead to the same goal. He advocated a religion of universal oneness and cosmopolitanism.
5. He emphasised universalism and brotherhood.
6. Perfection is already within us.

EDUCATIONAL PHILOSOPHY

1. All knowledge is within ourselves.
2. Child learns through self-education.
3. Education should be according to the need of children.
4. Concentration of mind is the essence of education. Everybody should be trained to develop the power of concentration and to practise chastity.
5. Education for all — National System of Education should begin by acquainting the child with the home, community, country, its customs and manners, culture and philosophy and then knowledge of the various civilisations.

6. Women's Education should be for character, courage and chastity. Religion is the centre of women's education.
7. True religious education must be taught to the child.

Concept of education

Education is manifestation of perfection within us. It is self — development. Education must develop the will, produce infinite energy, zeal, courage and patience.

Aims of Education

The aims of Education are physical development, mental development, vocational aim — all aiming perfection, promoting universal brotherhood and developing faith in oneself.

Curriculum

The curriculum should develop every aspect of the personality of the pupils. A synthesis between Science and Vedanta should be achieved by the study of Religion and philosophy for spiritual development and science for peace and progress of mankind. Arts should be taught for developing a sense of beauty. Study of languages should comprise of Common language, Regional language, Sanskrit, Social Sciences, History, Geography, Economics, Home Science, Psychology should be included.

Methods of Teaching

Method of teaching adopted should be concentration, discussion, contemplation, faith in oneself and reverence, individual guidance and counselling, and freedom.

Role of Teacher

The roles of the teacher, according to Swami Vivekananda are:

- Provider of suitable environment
- Attitude of worshipper
- Guide

The qualities of the teacher according to Swami Vivekananda are renouncement of personal gains, purity, love and sympathy for pupils. Swami Vivekananda states *"The only true teacher is he who can immediately come down to the level of the student and transfer his soul to the student's soul and see through the students' eyes and hear through his ears and understand through his mind. Such a teacher can really reach, and none else. Child is the pivotal point of Education."*

Contribution of Swami Vivekananda to Education

i. Spirit of humanism — Education should lead to the goal of realising God through love of humanity, self sacrifice and working for the upliftment of mankind.

ii. Free and compulsory education. Education is the birth right of every individual.

iii. National system of Education, which advocated the inclusion of a study of India's heritage, culture, arts, poetry, religion, history and languages.

iv. Women's education was essential for economic, social and educational reform of the country.

v. Equal educational opportunities was focussed upon and casteism and untouchability were attacked.

vi. Rama Krishna Mission — The starting of Ramakrishna Mission was the greatest contribution of Swami Vivekananda to the educational and social sphere.

vii. Vedanta society was established at San Francisco and many other centres.

Relevance of Swami Vivekananda's educational ideas in the present context

In the present age, when Human Resource Development has assumed an overwhelming significance, Swami Vivekananda's concept of Education as a 'man-making process' becomes more meaningful. Personality development and self-study, and promoting universal brotherhood are quite in consonance with the strategies for national development. Education for social upliftment and economic growth is quite in keeping with today's social problems and the need for creating social awareness.

RABINDRANATH TAGORE (1861-1941)

Biographical Sketch and Achievements

Family Background

Rabindranath Tagore was born in Calcutta. He was the fourteenth and youngest son of Maharshi Devendranath and grandson of prince Dwarkanath Tagore. The Tagore family was well-known for its progressive and enlightened views. The children were brought up in great simplicity.

Educational Background

Rabindranath studied the Upanishads, Astronomy and Sanskrit from his father. He attended the Seminary and Bengal Academy but could not adjust himself to the dead routine and lifeless teaching of the school. He revolted against the system of education. After private education,he was sent to England to study law but he returned.

Achievements

- Started writing for Bengali periodicals.
- Established the famous Shantiniketan at Bolpur, 95 miles from Calcutta in 1901. It developed into an important educational institution based on unconventional ideas.
- Rabindranath Tagore was awarded the Nobel Prizein 1913. He spent the amount he received (8000) onthe school.
- He visited Europe on many occasions, Japan, and United States.
- Accepted Knighthood in 1915 but renounced it as a protest in 1919 against the methods adopted for quelling Punjab.
- Established Vishvabharati, an international university with a view to bringing about understanding between eastern and western countries.

Tagore's Philosophy of Life

VEDANTIN

- God is all powerful and pervades in everything of the universe.
- The entire universe is the manifestation of Brahma. A Vedantin as he was, he believed in 'I am Brahma'.
- He believed in the Brotherhood of Man, Fatherhood of God and in the need for universal religion.

INDIVIDUALIST

- Individualist as he was, he believed in giving the right type of freedom to the individual and in catering to individual differences. Yet, there is unity in the fact that everything has *one source, one origin,* namely God.

IDEALIST

- Man should live for the ultimate Truth which liberates us from the cycle of birth and death and makes us one with the creator.

SPIRITUALIST

- Every individual should try to attain perfection spiritually. This will lead to better social order, human brotherhood, and finally to universal brotherhood.

HUMANIST

- Ultimate goal of life can be attained through an understanding of humanity.
- Absolute manifests itself in men. Reality is human. Truth is human.
- Humanity is a necessary factor in the perfection of divine truth.

NATURALIST

- Nature is a great teacher.
- Nature is Mother Nature - benevolent and generous.
- God revealed himself through various forms and colours of Nature.
- Education divorced from Nature has brought harm to children.

- Human being should have close communion with Nature.

INTERNATIONALIST

- World Brotherhood and world peace were the goals of Vishva Bharati.

Educational Ideas

Rabindranath Tagore was a practical educationist as evident by the Vishva Bharati established by him. His educational ideas were closely connected with his philosophy of life.

Basic principles

(i) **Harmony with all things** was one of the basic principlesof Tagore's philosophy. The highest education according to Tagore is that which makes our life in harmony with nature, human surroundings and international relations.

(ii) **Principles of freedom** - Child should be brought up in anatmosphere of freedom and liberty. Education has its meaning and object in freedom - freedom from ignorance, about the laws of the universe, freedom from passion and prejudice.

(iii) **Principles of creative expression** - Tagore assigned an important place to arts, crafts, music, drawing as education should promote creative self-expression.

(iv) **Active communication with nature and man**- If the child's education is in natural surroundings, it will help the child in developing the power of communication with nature.

Concept of Education

- **Education as enlightenment**: Education seeks to unfold allthat is good and noble in the individual. Education is an integral part of the adventure of life. It is a function of health and natural expression of the mind's vitality.
- **Education as a developmental process**: Education is development of the whole man. It is the process consisting of flowering the personality of children.

- **Education as harmony**: The highest education is not merelygiving information but makes our life" in harmony with all existence.

Aims of Education

The aims of education, according to Tagore were the following:

(i) Education or fullness.

(ii) Physical development.

(iii) Intellectual development

(iv) Development of the habits of constant curiosity and alertness of mind.

(v) Knowledge and assimilation of the essential scholarship of the culture of one's own country, cultivation of high values as simple living, high thinking, truth, good and beauty.

(vi) Making religion and morality an intimate part of life.

Curriculum

Rabindranath Tagore emphasises the need for a broad based curriculum covering all the aspects of child's life — physical intellectual, social, economic, aesthetic and spiritual may be developed.

(a) **Curriculum** included the following subjects, (i) Language, and Literature, Mother Tongue, other Indian Languages, English, Foreign languages like Russian, German, French, Latin and Chinese (ii) Mathematics (iii) Natural Sciences - Physics, Chemistry, Botany, Zoology, General Science and Health Education, (iv) Social Sciences — History, Geography, Economics and Sociology (v) Agricultural and Technical subject. (vi) Arts, Music, Dance (vii) Philosophy, Religion and Psychology.

(b) **Activities and Occupations** - (i) Dancing (ii) Dramatics (iii) Music (iv) Games and Sports (v) Drawing and Painting (vi) Agriculture and Gardening (vii) Excursions, (viii) Regional Study (ix) Laboratory work (x) Social Service and Self Government

(c) **Actual living and community service** — At Shanti Niketan, life is practical, full of life and vigour. Every one is an active member of the community and has to render service and manual labour. Department of Rural reconstruction is a centre of attraction.

Education must accord with life. It must not only derive the contents but also its substance and inspiration from social life at large.

Besides the comprehensive broad based curriculum, Rabindranath advocated the following:

(i) Education through emotions through performing and visual arts — striking a balance between education of nature and the education of man through art, music, dancing and painting.

(ii) Education through Mother Tongue.

(iii) Manual training for spiritual development.

(iv) Physical and social sciences for broadening the vision of the student.

Methods of teaching advocated were the following:

(i) Teaching while walking i.e. through excursion

(ii) Debate and discussion method

(iii) Heuristic method

(iv) Activity method

Discipline

Discipline, according to Rabindranath Tagore, grew from within. If punishment had to be resorted to, on rare occasions, it was done in a family spirit. School was considered to be a home.

Role of the teacher

The teacher was a guru. He guided and stimulated the students. He has to keep them on the right track. He has to understand the child and have a sympathetic attitude. According to Tagore "A lamp can never light another lamp unless it continuously tries to burn its own flame". He should not stop learning but must have a receptive and learning attitude.

Religious and spiritual education

Tagore believed that religious and spiritual education alone help an individual to realise himself. It will enable Man to communicate with God. The highest truth can be realised through meditation.

Women's education

Tagore stated "Woman should acquire pure knowledge for being a human being and utilitarian knowledge for becoming true woman."

Education of the masses (Universal Education)

Tagore felt that the masses suffered a lot due to Universal Education through Elementary or Primary Education and Social or Adult Education.

Tagore's contribution to education was Vishwabharati. The *main objectives* of creating Vishwabharati were:

(a) teaching the different cultures of the East.

(b) to establish the Institute of Rural Reconstruction.

(c) to establish a living relationship between East and West and promote inter-cultural and inter-social amity.

Tagore's Contribution to Education

The greatest contribution to education was Vishwabharati. Vishwabharati, the international university was established in 1921. The university, which evolved out of the practical implementation of Tagore's educational ideas at Shanti Niketan was established by Devendranath Tagore in 1901. Vishwabharati stood for harmonisation of the East and West in nature and spirit and symbolised universal brotherhood of the nations.

Vishwabharati was created with a view to teaching cultures of the East, to establishing an Institute of Rural reconstruction for achieving a happy human life in the villages and for unification of mankind.

The constituents of Vishwabharati were: (i) Shantiniketan school. (ii) the University (iii) Institute of Rural reconstruction. Shantiniketan was characterised by an atmosphere of joy and freedom, love and peace, sympathy and nobleness of spirit, simple living and high thinking and homely atmosphere. The school was in a natural setting resulting in spiritual development. The school was organised under huge trees and characterised by intimate contact between teacher and the taught. The school was self-sufficient and self- governing.

Vishwabharati reflects the ideals of Rabindranath Tagore. Vishwabharati comprised of Vidya Bhavan (school of research), Shiksha Bhavan (department for academic studies of a general nature), China Bhavan (institute for Indo-Chinese studies) Adhyapak Shiksha Bhavan (college for training perspective teachers), Kala Bhavan (institution for training in arts and crafts), Sangeeta Bhavan, Shilpa Bhavan, Hindi Bhavan and Islamic Research section.

The *features of Vishwabharati University* were as follows:

- Natural surrounding
- Co-educational and residential
- Cosmopolitan
- Homely and spiritual atmosphere
- Co-curricular activities
- Individual attention
- Perfect discipline
- Simple living and high thinking
- Unity of mankind

Institute of Rural reconstruction, the third section of Vishwabharati, was established with the following objectives in view,

- to impart knowledge about rural life and problems to the pupils
- to find out the problems and tackling them in a practical way,
- to promote a happy and contented life in the villages bydisseminating knowledge and experience
- to develop a practical all-round system of elementary education
- to develop sense of service and sacrifice, sense of their own intrinsic worth among the pupils, provision of practical experience in actual cultivation, farming, animal husbandry and other aspects of farmer in a spirit of cooperation and instruction in sciences.

Relevance in today's context

Rabindranath Tagore's naturalism is significant when we are faced with the problems of environmental degradation, need for conservation of natural resource and wild life. His humanism and principles of rural reconstruction are most useful and practical for the social development, and human resource enrichment. His internationalism gives the cue for global perspective, world peace and the concept of a World Family.

MAHATMA GANDHI (1869-1948)

Biographical Sketch

Family background

Mahatma Gandhi 'Father of the Nation' was born on 2nd October 1869. His father was the Prime Minister of Rajkot. At the age of 13, he was married to Kasturba.

Education

After passing his matriculation he went to England to study Law. He passed his law examination and was called to the Bar in 1891.

After his return from England he set up his practice in Rajkot.

Experience in South Africa

He went to South Africa for attending to the legal affairs of a rich firm. Being an Indian, he was thrown out of the first class compartment and had bitter experiences of racial discrimination. The fundamental ideals of his philosophy of life namely, Truth and Non-violence were evolved during this period.

Struggle for India's freedom

On his return to India, he took leading part in the freedom movement. He launched the Non-Cooperation Movement after Jallianwala Bagh atrocities. His Dandi March and Quit India Movement enkindled the national spirit in every Indian man, woman, and students of all levels.

Established Sabarmati Ashram and Sevagram Ashram

An idealist, who believed in a simple disciplined life spent in the upliftment of the poor, sick and down trodden. He established Sabarmati Ashram in 1915 and Sevagram Ashram in 1925. His ideals were reflected in his works Hind Swaraj and My Experiments with Truth.

Mahatma Gandhi's Philosophy of Life

Deeply influenced by the humanistic idealism of the past, the practical philosophy of the Bhagawad Geeta and the works of Leo Tolstoy, the principles of Mahatma Gandhi's philosophy of life were as follows:

- God is ultimate reality, the arbitrator of our fate, the living law governing the whole universe. He is the undefinable, mysterious power that pervades every thing. God is life, Truth, Light and Love.
- Truth is all-pervading and can be realised only through Truth, through a way of life characterised by strict discipline, austerity, non violence, sense of humility and Ahimsa.
- Non violence is a positive and dynamic virtue i.e resistance to evil through love.
- Satyagraha is belief in Truth, power of Truth and love by which evil is overcome by self-suffering and self-sacrifice.
- Spiritual society is characterised by realisation of the Absolute by moving towards human brotherhood. It is based on principles of love, non-violence, truth, justice. It will be free from exploitation and injustice. There will be no conflict between individual and society. All will move towards the common goal of Truth. Service unto Man, Service unto God will lead to realisation of Truth or God.
- Spirituality can be carried to the masses only through bread. Material possessions are only means, not ends.

Mahatma Gandhi propounded a philosophy of life based on Truth and Non-Violence and practised it.

Mahatma Gandhi's Philosophy of Education

All the characteristic features of Mahatma Gandhi's philosophy of life were translated into action in his philosophy of education.

Meaning of education

The concept of education according to the Mahatma Gandhi is explicit in his definition of education. *"By education I understand an all round drawing out of the best in the child and man - body, mind and spirit."*

Literacy is itself not education. It is only a means to education. Literacy training in school is not education as more emphasis is laid on tools on the personality development of the educand. Education which draws out the best or Truth consists of the development of the mind and body with an awakening of the soul.

Aims of Education

The two sets of aims of education are immediate and ultimate. The immediate aims comprise of bread and butter aim, cultural aim, harmonious development of all powers, moral or character development and aim of liberating the educand. The ultimate aim leads to self-realisation, the knowledge of Truth and God in one's life.

Curriculum

Craft-centred education is the only means to train the whole man leading to the highest development of the man and soul. A manual and product craft was to be chosen. It was the starting point of all other subjects and the meeting point of physical and social sciences.

The *salient features of Craft-centred Education were*:

i. Stress was laid on the principles of co-operative activity, accuracy of planning, initiative and individual responsibility in learning.

ii. Teaching signifies provision of useful experiences and activity and correlation of subjects.

iii. Craft-centred education leads to richness and fullness of culture.

iv. Craft saves people from exploitation, selfishness and team-work while retaining the individuality.

v. It makes education self-supporting.

vi. Positive relationship between education and life could be established as craft selected in the school is craft of the locality.

vii. Basic education Scheme propagated by Mahatma Gandhi comprised of (a) Basic craft in accordance with local condition (b) Mother Tongue, (c) Arithmetic (d) Social Studies (e) General Science (f) Art (g) Music (h) Domestic Science for girls. These subjects are to be taught with craft as the centre of correlation.

Discipline

Real discipline comes from self-discipline that arises spontaneously from the inner springs of life rather than that which is imposed by external sources. Self-discipline arises from a pure life of self-restraint, fearlessness, usefulness and self-sacrifice. Social discipline emerges out of conjoint co-operatives encouraged by craft-centred education.

Role of the teacher

The teacher is more important than the textbook in the free development of the child. The teacher should provide the free, fearless learning environment for the child. The teacher should set an example by his own values and attitudes.

Contribution of Mahatma Gandhi to Education

Basic education in other words, craft — centred education is the greatest contribution of Mahatma Gandhi to Education. The salient features of Basic Education were as follows.

i. Free and compulsory education within the ages of 7 and 14.

ii. Mother tongue as the medium of instruction.

iii. Craft as the centre of education. Inculcation of values through craft was the main objective of craft-centred education. Education of the hand, head and heart was achieved through craft-centred education. The values developed were co-operation dignity of labour, accuracy, organisation of work, initiative, sense of responsibility and equality.

iv. Basic education is based on the principle *Learn while you Earn, and Earn while you Learn.* Self sufficiency was the fundamental principle. The state should provide the facilities for production and marketing.

v. Cult of Non-Violence was the ideological background of Basic education. Every act should be characterised by love and freedom. Boys and girls will study together like brothers and sisters in freedom and self-imposed restraint.

vi. Basic education lays the foundation of ideal citizenship.

vii. The psychological principles of Basic education were:

- Child centred education
- Learning by doing
- Play and creative work
- Utilisation of instincts
- Correlation
- Life-centred education
- Love and sympathy.

In the words of Mahatma Gandhi, " The age of Basic education includes the education of the whole society beginning with the children and going upto adults and old men and women. It has to be imparted through the practice of handicrafts, village sanitation and medical relief, preventive and curative."

In the words of Dr. Patel, "Gandhiji's philosophy of education is naturalistic in its setting, idealistic in its aim and pragmatic in its method and programme of work. All these tendencies are not separate in his philosophy. They fuse into a unity, giving rise to a theory of education which would suit the need of the day and the loftiest aspiration of the human soul."

Relevance in the present context

A synthesis of naturalism, idealism and pragramatism and sound psychologically, sociologically and biologically, the main objective of Gandhijis educational ideas is social upliftment and economic growth through productive activity based on the ideals of Truth and Non-Violence. In the present context, human resource development and enhanced productivity are the needs of the hour, to combat poverty, unemployment, and social injustice. So the fundamental principles of Basic education are the origin of techno-pedagogy and vocationalisation of education.

MAHARSHI KARVE (1858-1962)

BIOGRAPHICAL SKETCH

Family Background

Dhondo Keshav Karve, the champion of Women's Education was born on April 18, 1858. It was a significant year in the history of India as British. India was established in this year. His father, Keshopant Karve belonged to a high class wealthy family of Murud. As a result of the aristocratic habits of the predecessors of the family, the wealth was not maintained and Keshopant and his two brothers had to be satisfied with the small piece of land each one got of the ancestral property. So the family had to encounter economic problems.

Keshopant and his wife, Lakshmibai had six children out of which, three survived, namely, Dhondu's brother, Dhondu and his sister, Amba. The family had to live with meagre means and face many difficulties. However the high sense of self-respect and the glow of their noble family illumined their lives and was passed on to the children. The children learnt to face hardships and lead austere life with a high sense of discipline, industriousness and frugality. The impact of the rare qualities of his parents and the hard lessons learnt in childhood paved the way for the mission that Dhondo Keshav was to take up later.

Early Education

Besides these traits that Dhondu had inherited, he developed the habit to learning by heart and reciting slokas from various works. This capacity to recite eloquently in a clear voice attracted the attention of his teachers in the primary school. He had a great yearning to learn English and a keen interest in Mathematics. He worked hard and developed along with his brother.

Overcoming great hurdles and undertaking perilous journey and undaunted by his setback at Satara, he successfully completed his sixth standard examination at Kolhapur along with his cousin.

Even as a child at the primary school level his diligence and willingness to work was greatly appreciated. He was involved in the social education project started by his teacher at the Durgadevi temple at Murud. He was asked to read newspapers to the people. Later on, his teacher started a co-operative stores and Dhondu was asked to manage the selling and keep accounts.

Dhondu develops his personality

He started regular religious worship and reading of religious books. Thus he got mental strength. His pastimes of climbing trees, collecting gooseberries and swimming gave him physical strength.

Dondo Karve's settlement in Bombay

With a group of friends he came to Bombay and got admission in Robert Money School. He passed his Matriculation Examination. Hardly a year after he came to Bombay, he lost his father. As it was not possible for him to go and visit his family, he met them during Diwali and discussed the future of the family with his mother and brother.

During his school days, he met Narharpant Joshi, who became his long term friend and companion.

Family Commitment

After the demise of his father, he assisted his brother and mother by working from dawn to dusk with tuitions with hardly any time for rest or pleasure.

He stayed with his friend, who later brought his wife. Mr Karve too brought his wife, Radhabai and his two and a half year old son. The joint family establishment comprised a Mr. Joshi, his wife, his son, four boarders brought by Mr. Karve from Murud and Mr. Kale and his wife Radhabai. His wife had learnt Marathi and Mr. Karve taught her English. She worked with patience, silently and managed the household. However it became too much for her even though her sister came to stay with them. She expired. Though it was an agonising situation Mr. Karve carried on with his schedule.

Teaching Career

Mr. Karve graduated from Elphinstone College with outstanding personalities like Gopalkrishna Gokhale the Great mathematician, Chimanbhai Setalvad.

He became a teacher and taught in reputed schools. He joined the Maratha High School. He worked with zeal and commitment and won the appreciation of his superiors.

He joined the Ferguson college as Professor of Mathematics and became a life member of the Deccan Education Society.

Social Commitment

His zeal for contributing to the cause of education made him start the Murud Fund and Maratha five percent fund by setting aside a part of his meagre income as a teacher for the cause of education.

He was constantly perturbed by the conditions of the widows and the hardships they had to go through. He has seen the widows in his family and his friend's family. The widow Remarriage Act was passed but still the women who lost their husbands were persecuted and harassed in society.

Setting up institutions and collecting funds

He started the Anath Balika Ashram at Hingne where widows were educated. Prof. Karve was inspired by the work done by Pandit Vidyasagar in Bengal. Publications like '*Indu Prakash*', the articles and poems written to build public opinion furnished a lot of information on the movement.

Prof. Karve sets an example

Since Radhabai's death, her memories frequently haunted him and disturbed his mind. His friends father had discussed with him regarding his future. Finally, he decided to set a personal example in the field of social reform. So he married Godubai, a widow Narharpant's younger sister. She was renamed as Anandibai. The marriage was opposed and Mr. Karve and his family were boycotted.

Widow marriage association was started by Vishnushastri Pandit and Prof. Karve was the secretary. The name of the Association was changed to Association for the Removal of Restrictions to the Marriage of widows.

Prof. Karve had great admiration for Pandita Ramabai who had started and led Sharda Sadan to progress. Prof. Karve's second wife was trained here and the spirits of social service was ingrained in her and her companions. In 1896, the Anath Balika Ashram Association was started. Dr. Bhandarkar was the President and Prof. Karve was the Secretary. He collected funds from all possible sources and gave his own Insurance Policy for the Ashram.

The *Mahila Vidyalaya* was started in a humble way in 1907 by a monthly contribution of a philanthrophist. This was called *Brahmacharya Fund.* The *Nishkama Karma Math* was started where the value of self-less service was practised. The Math was severely criticised.

After retiring from his Professorship he devoted his time fully to the Ashram. He evolved the proposal of a separate University for women and it materialised in 1916. The S.N.D.T. University is a magnum opus of his contribution to education.

Philosophy of life

At every stage from his own education to the establishment of institutions, life was full of hardships, adjustments, and challenges. His philosophy of life is epitomised in the fact that Dhondo Keshav Karve was honoured with the honorary degree of D.Litt by University of Poona, Benaras University and S.N.D.T. University. In 1957 the University of Bombay conferred the Honorary degree of Dr. of Laws on him. On Republic Day 1958, the list of awards of Bharat Ratna was headed by his name. He was known all the world over as Maharshi Karve.

The salient features of the philosophy of his life were:

- Devotion to work and studies
- Quest for knowledge and truth
- Undaunted determination
- Tenderness and sensitivity to others' sufferings
- Experience enables one to regard success as well as failure with indifference.
- To be a good and do good things
- Sacrifice, mutual help, affection and devotion as a base for any task
- Tolerance, fearlessness, rational outlook and maintaining equanimity against heavy odds
- Zeal for spread of education
- Faith, steady confidence and perseverance.
- Gratefulness for sympathy and support
- Fight for equality all over the world
- There is probably no unmixed evil or unmixed good in the world. Even calamities have their useful function.

- To regard a good man or a great man as a human being striving to reach the highest pinnacle of righteousness is a far greater tribute to his worth than to worship him as a divine incarnation.
- He does not believe in a God who dwells apart from the universe and guides the destinies of human beings but has fixed his faith in a Supreme Being which pervades the universe.
- He did not have a religion but had a religious spirit. The religious spirit in men enabled them to purify themselves and to strive to reach the ideal of perfection. The yearning to purify oneself, to lift oneself and to be perfect has been the goal of Maharshi Karve's life.
- He did not consider it important whether a man is in the right or wrong, he has sympathy and admiration for those who choose a line of thinking after careful and independent deliberation
- Inspite of his stern detachment and crowded hours he loved the fleeting things of life.
- He believed his life and achievements were not anything outstanding but the outcome of circumstances he worked in and the opportunities he had. His life was more of giving than taking.
- He states "If there is any truth in the idea of rebirth and if the particular form of rebirth is shaped by the desirea man's heart is occupied with, I pray that the Ruler of the universe may enable to serve during all my succeeding births the same cause I have been able to serve during this one and that my devotion for it may increase with every birth."

EDUCATIONAL PHILOSOPHY

Concept of Education

Education should teach self-reliance. Every man or women should acquire knowledge and skills to enable one to stand on one's own legs. Education of widows and marriage of widows are separate issues.

Aims of Education

The principal aim of education for women should be to equip them with a training that would make them efficient housewives and mothers. Women should occupy a distinct status of their own from that of men. Women are an integral part of the social organism to the same extent as men are but the office or their role is different. Though equal, it is perhaps greater in importance. Education has to prepare them for these roles.

Content

The medium of instruction has to be mother tongue. The curriculum should be adapted to their special needs and conditions retaining the simplicity of Indian style of living. The content should enable them to acquire a good moral foundation for their lives and character.

Discipline

He believed in strict discipline with sacrifice and social service without expectation of material benefits. It should be characterised by reason and flexibility.

Teacher

The teacher should stimulate thinking, and inculcate the value of discipline with tenderness, affection and a sympathetic attitude. The teacher must infuse tenacity, courage, determination and develop will-power by setting an example of hard work with a definite goal. Just as Maharshi Karve was, the teacher must be delicate like a flower and harder than a thunderbolt.

Maharshi Karve's life has been a lesson of idealism, endless activity and a high sense of morality. The secret of his long life was his regular habits.

RELEVANCE IN PRESENT CONTEXT

In the present context, women's education leading to participation of women in national development is the main thrust of the educational policy. Equal status of the girl-child is the basic principle of the national policy on women. It may be rightly said that the principles of women's education enunciated by Maharshi Karve are the foundations of women's education and the roots of the multi-faceted and multi-disciplinary courses provided by S.N.D.T. Women's University. The principle that an educated woman is the nucleus of an educated family was amply illustrated by the roles played by Maharshi Karve's wife Anandibai and his daughter-in-law, Iravati Karve in the development of the institutions established by him from their very inception.

CONTRIBUTION TO WOMEN'S EDUCATION

- The fundamental principles of upliftment and empowerment of women through education.
- Education for self-reliance providing knowledge and skills for standing on one's own legs.
- Education for enabling them to become efficient housewives and mother.
- Education through mother tongue and according to their special needs.
- Concept of a Women's University.

JOHN DEWEY (1859-1952)

John Dewey, the most distinguished American thinker influenced the American schools as well as the educational movements in the Far East and in Russia. Dewey was a great educationist and philosopher.

Biographical Sketch

John Dewey was born in Vermont in 1859. His father was an ordinary shopkeeper. He was brought up in a rural environment.

In 1879, he graduated from Vermont University. He obtained the degree of Ph.D. in Philosophy from John Hopkins University.

He was a lecturer in the University of Michigan for some time. In 1894, he was appointed Head of the Department of Philosophy in the University of Chicago.

His philosophical doctrines and ideology of Education were the outcome of the influence of the industrial revolution, the change of population, and the accelerated development of mechanisation and democratic ideals.

In Chicago he founded the University Laboratory school in 1896. He desired that this school should have the same relation to the Department of Philosophy as psychological laboratory to the Department of Psychology and science laboratory to the Department of Science. The purpose of the laboratory school was to obtain knowledge of facts and laws unknown to educationists and to test those theories by conducting experiments of a novel nature. The laboratory schools and the experiments conducted gained popularity far and wide. So he was invited by the University of Peking to deliver lectures on Philosophy and Education for a period of two years. Later on, the National Government of Turkey assigned him the task of drawing up a report on the reorganisation of national schools in Turkey. From 1904-1930 he was professor of Philosophy and Education at the Columbia University.

His Writings

John Dewey's educational philosophy and practice were effectively expounded in his works. The most important of his works were the following: (1) School and Society (2) Democracy and Education (3) Schools of Tomorrow (with Evelyn Dewey) (4) My Pedagogic Creed (5) The Child and the Curriculum (6) How we think? (7) Reconstruction in Philosophy (8) Interest and Effort in Education (9) Human Nature and Conduct : An introduction to Social Psychology (10) Experience and Nature (11) The Quest for certainty: A study of the relation of knowledge and action (12) Sources of Science of Education (13) Education Today (14) Freedom and Culture.

Philosophy of Life

Dewey was a pragmatist and his views were characterised by practicality and utility. As indicated by his laboratory school, no principle was accepted without the hypothesis being tested with the help of experiments. The salient features of his philosophy were the following:

i. **Concept of Philosophy**: Philosophy is not a passive contemplation. It reflects life and solves problems. It is a social subject. It is a study of social conflicts, especially those involved in the relation of the three leading forces of modern society viz. democracy, industry and science. The problem of philosophy is to clarify men's ideas regarding the social and moral strifes of the times.

ii. **Concept of Values:** There are no fixed absolute values which are eternal. Values are relative and changing.

Man creates his own values with intelligence and creative power.

iii. **Views on Reality:** Reality is that which evolves out of the experience of man in his physical and social environment. It is relative to man, time and place. So it is changing and still in the making.

iv. **Truth is Utility:** Whatever fulfils man's purpose and developes his life is Truth. Truth and utility are identical.

v. **Thought and Action:** Action is superior to thought. Thought and action are inseparable and complementary to each other.

vi. **Concept of Democracy:** Democracy was one of the fundamental principles of Dewey's philosophy. Democracy means co-operative activity. It is a mode of associated living. It is concerned with the welfare and interests of the all the members of the group. The mode of action is through group interaction. Democracy ensures equality of opportunity to all. Consequently, an ideal society is one in which everyone is thinking and acting and contributing towards the common well-being.

vii. **Relationship between Individual and Society:** An individual grows and develops in society which is indispensable for the development of the personality of the individual. So there is an organic relationship between individual and society.

viii. **Instrumental Philosophy:** Every activity in life is an instrument for achieving some goal which improves life. Ideas are instruments for solving the problem of life.

ix. **Experimental Philosophy:** All of us are carrying out experiments consciously or unconsciously and trying to solve our problems. Experience is the core of life. Every idea should be tested by experiment before it is accepted.

x. **Emphasis on Science and Scientific Methods:** Experimental method is the most scientific method of investigation into problems of human affairs.

EDUCATIONAL PHILOSOPHY

Concept of Education

Definition of Education:"*It is the development of all those capacities of the individual which will enable him to control his environment and fulfil his possibilities.*"

Characteristics of Education

(a) **Education has two sides — the psychological side** is the study of the child i.e his instincts and innate powers. Child is the starting point of education.

Sociological side — emphasises the need of the social conditions in which the child is to live and grow for the society to which he belongs. *All education proceeds by participation of the individual in social consciousness of the race.*

(b) **Education is life** — Education is not a preparation of life but life itself. Life is a by-product of activities and education is the offspring of these activities. Education must give opportunity to the child to face various problems of actual life. Life does not mean individual life but social life.

(c) **Education is growth** — Education is the process of growth. Growth unlimited and illimitable is the true objective of education. Education should enable the individual to grow to his maximum capacity. The teacher should facilitate this process.

(d) **Education is social efficiency** — Education signifies the social continuity of life. Education enables Man to develop reasoning, social relations and become socially efficient. Social efficiency includes economic and cultural efficiency.

(e) **Education is continuous reconstruction of experiences** — Education is a process of living through continuous reconstruction of experiences. Education is by experience, for experience and of experience. Experience is the only source of knowledge. Education constantly reorganises experiences, preserves valuable experiences and reorganises them according to new demands. The goal of regulation and organisation of learning experiences and activities should be the creation of a better society. Continuous reconstruction and reorganisation of experiences is necessary for helping man to grow physically, mentally, socially and morally.

Aims of Education

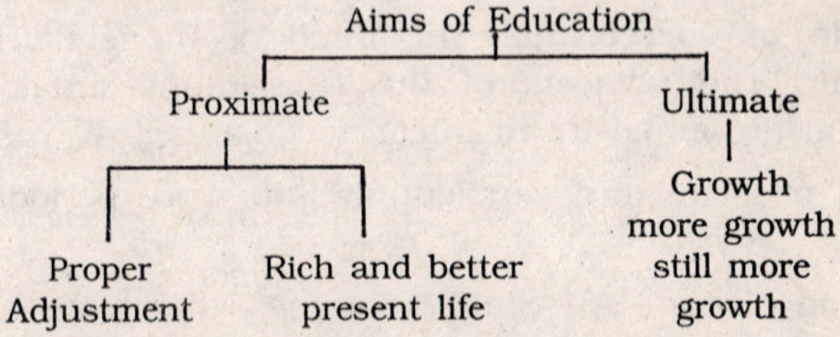

"Education means enterprise of supplying the conditions which ensure growth of adequacy of life."

Curriculum

According to Dewey, the main criteria for constructing the curriculum **were the** child's interests, instincts and abilities.

The principles underlying the construction of curricula were:

Principle of utility: The subjects included in the curriculum must be useful in solving human problems and facing life situations. Elaborating further, he stated "Man's fundamental common concern about food, shelter, clothing, household furnishing and the appliances commended with production, exchange and consumption."

Principle of flexibility: The curriculum should be flexible rather than rigid and predetermined. It must be capable of accommodating changes in the child's interests and inclinations and must be according to social requirements. At the elementary stage, the curriculum should cater to the four fold interests of the child, viz., (1) conservation and communicating, (2) enquiry and curiosity to find out things, (3) construction, and (4) artistic expression.

Principle of child's experience: The curriculum should be organised in a manner suited to enrichment of the experiences already acquired and add new experiences and ideas to the existing ones. Teaching through books should be supplemented by programmes which provide a variety of practical experiences.

Principle of community-centredness and life-centredness: Dewey believed that the demands of the community should be fulfilled through the agencies of education. Hence problem of life should form part of the curriculum.

Principle of correlation: The mind of the child is a complete unit. The subjects of the curriculum should be correlated and presented in an integrated manner.

Division of elementary curriculum into three periods as follows:

First period (From 4 - 8 years)	Simple reading, writing, arithmetic, ordinary farm work.
Second period (From 8 - 12 years)	Social studies, Experimental science.
Third period (12 years onwards)	Problems of agriculture, consumption, production, transportation, exchange and distribution.

Methods of teaching

The principles that he advocated for selecting the methods of teaching were as follows:

Principle of child's interests: Child is the centre of education. So the focus of methods of teaching is the child's interest and faculties. The genuine principle of interest is the principle of re-organised identity of the proposed line of action with the self that it lies in the direction of agents in self-expression.

Principle of learning through activity: Learning takes place through purposeful activity and actual life experiences. Every child should participate in purposeful activity and gain life experiences. The teacher should present the activity through personal problems which will appeal to the children. Thus, the school will be transformed into a dynamic living society where each one's contribution is welcomed.

Emphasis on self-education, play-way and creative self-expression: Self-education enables the child to learn in his own way. Play-way method creates interest in the child. Every child has the power of self-expression. So Dewey emphasised self education, play-way method and creative self-expression.

Project and problem method: Project method provides all the conditions of a good learning process. It is a purposeful activity chosen from the real life of children and proceeding in a social environment. It facilitates learning through the activity. It provides opportunities for work and play. The steps involved in project method are - (a) providing a situation, (b) choosing a project, (c) planning, (d) executing, and (e) judging and evaluating.

According to the problem method, the subjects of the curriculum are divided into small units. These units are presented to the child in the form of problems pertaining to the child.

Thus, both the methods emphasise pupil's purposes, needs, interests and self-activity.

Concept of Discipline

Dewey emphasised social discipline. The individual capabilities of the child can develop only in a society. Discipline emanates from co-operation. Discipline should not be enforced but should be from within. Conduct and discipline should be developed keeping the requirements of the society in view. Dewey's views on discipline are expressed in the following words:

"Out of doing things that are to produce results and out of doing in a social and co-operative way, there is born a discipline of its own kind and type."

Discipline arising out of doing things in a social and co-operative way will inculcate right attitudes, interests, morals, character and other qualities of head and heart necessary for democratic living. The natural impulses of the child can be directed and disciplined by co-operative activities of the school.

Role of the teacher

According to Dewey, the teacher plays an important role in the education of the child. His task is to guide and supervise the educative activities of the children and secure the maximum development in a social atmosphere. He cultivates social attitudes, social patterns and social interests in them and lays the foundations of a good life by his sympathetic behaviour and direct contact with the pupils. Teacher is a representative of God in society. The teacher should have freedom to frame curriculum and to carry on administration of the school keeping the interests of the child and society in mind. The teacher who has vast experience has a right to make suggestions as to what to do.

Concept of an Ideal School

It is the place where the child learns by his experiences. It is a society in miniature. It is a socio-psychological necessity. In the words of Dewey, "The school is simply that form of community life in which all these agencies are concentrated that will be most effective in bringing the child to share in the inherited sources of the inherited race and to use his own process for social end".

The **characteristic features of an ideal school** are as follows:-

1. It is an *enlarged family and enlarged ideal home* where the training is more perfect with more scientific guidance and better equipment. The atmosphere of love and affection that prevails at home shouid also be found in the school. It should preserve, continue and rebuild the child's home activities.
2. The ideal school is a *society in miniature.* It cultivates social consciousness and social loyalty in the pupils. It interacts with other agencies and provides adequate opportunities for the child to construct and reconstruct his experiences.
3. It is a *child-centred institution* which focusses on needs, interests and potentialities of the child.
4. It is a place for experimentation for both the teachers and the taught. *Classrooms are treated as laboratories and teachers as demonstrators.*
5. Provision for *vocational education in one skill* is made. The skill is selected on the basis of the needs of society.
6. *Moral Education* is given through activities performed jointly with others and proper relations with them.
7. *Learning by doing* is the motto of the ideal school.
8. There should be *free discipline* in the school. The natural impulses of the child should be directed through co-operative activities of the school.

Thus the ideal school is a replica of society.

Contribution to Education

John Dewey's greatest contribution was the concept of Democracy in Education and the intimate relationship that he established between the individual and society. His emphasis on the construction and reconstruction of experiences and the democratic values of freedom of the child and free discipline brought about a changed progressive outlook on education. The importance given by him to experimentation in education sowed the seeds of Action Research and widened the horizons of Educational Psychology. He brought about a radical change in the concept of education. The Ideal School which was a miniature democratic society was a live model of Democracy in Education.

The aims of education, according to Dewey, emphasised the development of the individual and the society in which he lives and inculcation of democratic values.

The principles of curriculum construction stated by him were a valuable contribution and provide guidelines for curriculum designers. The curriculum suggested by him are of great significance for social, economic and cultural development and nation-building. The philosophical, psychological and sociological factors of curriculum construction are given their due importance.

His views regarding discipline and his concept of self-government in schools formed the basis of democratisation of schools.

Thus the principles of education formulated by John Dewey are the key concepts of Education for Democracy. John Dewey revolutionised education by synthesising individual and social aims of education and providing a new perspective of schools as training ground for building a democratic society. His greatest contribution was Project and Problem Method advocated by him.

Relevance to Present Context

In a socialist democratic country which is endeavouring to build a democratic learning society, the concept of education and the aims of education are very relevant. The methods of teaching suggested and the model of Ideal School given by him are good examples capable of providing valuable guidelines for the progressive schools of today. His emphasis on varied activities to develop social skills and social efficiency, and principles of self-government in schools are of great use to educationists even today. Though quite a number of these principles are being implemented in some of the schools, yet the development of creativity and problem-solving abilities among the pupils leaves much to be desired in many of the schools. The Schools Improvement Projects are working on these lines but the experiments have to be conducted on a large scale involving more schools of different categories so that all strata of society benefit by it.

ROUSSEAU (1712-1778)

Jean Jacques Rousseau, a pioneer of the Naturalist School of educational thought, one of the revolutionary writers, who germinated the French Revolution, emerged from the vagrant life of a vagabond without literary training. He enunciated the system of education, free from intervention and rigidity. Rousseau's Naturalism was the outcome of his own life experiences and the political situations prevalent at that time.

BIOGRAPHICAL SKETCH

Jean Jacques Rousseau was born in the family of a poor watchmaker. His mother died soon after his birth, so he had very little formal education. He entered the world of work as an apprentice with an engineer. Being a victim of ill-treatment at the hands of his employer, he ran away as a vagabond without any attachment or sense of responsibility. During this period, his life was full of misdeeds. As he grew up, he became sober and at Geneva, he led a simple and pure life. He tried his hand at many occupations like private tutor, music teacher, composer and dramatist. Finally, he established as a successful writer at the age of 38. His writings sowed the seeds of the French Revolution. His works were:

- The progress of the Arts and Sciences
- The origin of inequality among men
- Social contract
- Emile or concerning education.

His writings embodied his views on the then prevalent social injustice and the rigid school discipline which deprived the children of their rightful natural freedom. His work **Emile** propagated his ideal on theory and practice of education. He was called the Father of Modern Educational Theory and Practice.

He died in Paris in 1778.

PHILOSOPHY OF LIFE

The social and political set-up of his times, the cruelty, hypocrisy and despotism prevalent then had aroused the feeling of discontent and wrath in him. The upsurge of revolutionary spirit gave rise to his philosophy of life.

The *fundamental concepts* of his philosophy were:

- Natural State
- Natural Man
- Natural Civilisation

Natural State is a simple farming community or state without the evils of large cities, namely, corruption, social classes and luxury.

Natural Man is guided and directed by his own nature. Man would have been happier if he had been allowed to remain in his natural state. According to him *Cities are the graves of civilisations and human institutions are one mass of folly and contradiction.*

Natural Civilisation is free from artificial surroundings and rigid barriers.

CONCEPTS OF NATURE

- Children have to be saved from the evil influences of society and brought about by laws of nature.
- Nature means the primitive emotions, instinctive judgement, natural instincts or innate tendencies of the child. *Nature means natural tendencies.* These natural tendencies are better bases for action than the experience gained by the child from the society.
- *Nature means contact with natural environment.* Child should be brought up in natural environment and he will automatically become a rational being. He will act according to the voice of his conscience.

EDUCATIONAL PHILOSOPHY

Concepts of Education

- Education is the development of the child's natural powers and abilities from within.
- The sources of education are (a) Nature, (b)Men and (c) Things. Education from men and things, that is, from social contacts and from experience of dealing with things in our physical surroundings, are inferior to education from Nature, i.e. from the education arising out of the spontaneous development and expansion of the child's natural tendencies and interests.

Kinds of Education

- **Preventive Education**: It means isolating the child from society and bringing him up by laws of Nature.
- **Negative Education**: It means guarding the heart against vice and mind against error. In the words of Rousseau, *"I call negative education that which tends to perfect the organs that are the instruments of knowledge and endeavours to prepare the way for reason by proper exercise of the senses."* A negative education does not mean the time of idleness, far from it. It does not give virtue, it protects from vice. It does not inculcate truth, it protects from error.

The characteristics of Negative Education are

a. **Protest against saving time**: Time lost on play and recreational activities in childhood is time spent on reconstruction of experiences. It is education. So it is really time profitably gained.

b. **Protest against book learning**: According to Rousseau, books are the cause of child's misery. By relieving school children of books and courses, we can take away the cause of their misery.

c. **Protest against formal lessons**: Rousseau stated, *"Get rid of the lesson and we get rid of their sorrow."* Emphasising application of knowledge, Rousseau challenged Formal Education by his statement, *"Give me a child of five who knows nothing and I shall return him to you knowing as much as those who have been under* *instruction from infancy with the difference that your pupil only knows things by heart while mine knows how to use his knowledge."*

d. **Protest against habit formation**: The only habit which the child should be allowed to form is to contract no habits. Children must be free and no restrictions must be placed on their activities. Children should form natural habits.

e. **No direct moral education**: No moral training should be given. Children should be allowed to get moral training from the natural consequences of their actions.

f. **Undoing current practices, Back to Nature**: Rousseau was very unhappy with the then prevalent practices. He stated, *"Man was once happy, now he is miserable. Undo what has been done and he will be happy once again"*.

Positive Education: Rousseau did not favour positive education as it tends to form the mind prematurely and to instruct the child in duties that belong to man (as an adult). It is unnatural, inhuman and opposed to the spontaneous development of the child. The characteristics of Positive Education are - (a) Stress on verbalism, (b) Emphasis on duty, strict discipline, (c) Undue importance of morality, religion and formation of habits.

Aims of Education and Curriculum

The most important aim of education is the natural development of the child's inner faculties and powers. Education should help the child to live, to work, to develop and utilise the various parts of the body, the sense organs and his powers properly. It should make the child a human being before he becomes a professional.

The aim of education should be different at different stages and the curriculum also changes according to the stage of development. Thus, according to the four stages of development, the aims and the curriculum for the four stages were as follows:

Stage	Aims and Curriculum
1. Infancy stage (upto five years)	To develop well-regulated freedom according to the capacities of the child. No formal teaching, constant exercise to make the child strong and proper protection of the child.
2. Childhood stage (5 to 12 years)	To develop sufficient strength in the child for having well-regulated freedom. Negative education, concentration on physical exercise as Childhood is the sleep of reason and the educator is not to disturb him in his sleep.
3. Boyhood stage (12 to 15 years)	a. To develop the intellect of the child. b. To enable him to meet the practical needs of life by acquiring the relevant knowledge. Physical Sciences, Languages, Mathematics Manual work, Trade, Social relations, Music, Drawing.
4. Adolescence	a. To enable him to live for others and to live together in social relationships. b. To enable him to sublimate his instincts. c. To achieve emotional, moral and religious development. Moral Science, Religion, History, Geography, Sex Education, Physical sciences, Aesthetics.

While discussing the curriculum at the various stages of development, the objectives of teaching certain subjects at the Boyhood and Adolescent stages are stated in the following manner:

Boyhood stage

The teaching of drawing is to achieve the objective of training the muscles and co-ordination of the eyes.

The teaching of sciences will develop heuristic attitude. The objective of teaching Mathematics is to develop precise thinking.

Social Sciences are to be taught with the objective of developing the value of co-operation and making them understand the need for co-operation and economic inter-dependence of man.

Adolescent stage

The main objective during this stage is to enable him to tackle situations in life. It had, therefore, to be taught through activities, not through lecture. Valuės had to be caught, not taught.

The aim of teaching history was to make the pupil understand the events not merely as facts and dates but from the point of view of values and moral development through examples of historical personalities.

The specific aim of teaching religious education was to enable the pupil to realise the existence of God. Sex education was to be imparted with a view to enlightening the pupil about sex affairs. Aesthetics was to be taught for cultivation and improvement of tastes.

Methods of Teaching

In accordance with his naturalistic philosophy, he laid stress on direct experience of things and on the principle of learning by doing. He advocates the heuristic method and condemns the use of textbooks. Regarding the methods of teaching religion and morals, Rousseau states, "It is by doing good that one becomes good. Occupy your pupil with all the good actions that are in his reach, let the interests of the poor always be his, let him assist them not only with purse, but his personal attention, let him serve them, protect them and consecrate to them his person and his time, let him be their advocate, he will never have nobler employment". He advocated practical activities like visits to shop and factories and work places for learning about social relations.

The principles of teaching which he advocated were the following:

- *Learning by doing* — It enables participation in activities in a natural way. This principle will give the child the pleasure of creative activity.

- *Direct experience* — According to Rousseau, knowledge gained from books is second hand and is easily forgotten. Knowledge acquired from learning situations is permanent. Rousseau urged experience before expression and objects before words.
- *Heuristic method* — In this method, the child is placed in the position of a discoverer. He is to be given an opportunity to make experiments with the apparatus prepared or invented by the pupil himself.
- *Method of individual instruction* — Individual instruction was stressed by Rousseau because it facilitates recognition of the individuality of the child.
- *Example is better than precept* — This axiom was given for imparting moral education. The teacher should set the example by practising morality. The teacher should provide opportunities to practise virtue.
- **Social relationship by social participation** — Social skills as establishing relationship are to be developed by visits to places where pupils come in contact with members of the community.

Concept of Discipline

Rousseau's slogan was *'Leave the child free'*. There should be absence of restraint. He advocated discipline by natural consequences. He stated *'Allow the child to suffer the natural consequences of his acts'*. For example, if he puts his hand in fire, let him burn his hand and learn by consequences.

Role of the teacher

The teacher had to remain in the background, provide suitable opportunities to enable free development of their interests. The teacher should protect the child from repressions, mental conflicts and mental disorders of any kind.

Education of Women

While the education of men was discussed with the example of an imaginary character *Emile*, the education of women was discussed with the example of *Sophy* who had to be the ideal wife of Emile. His views on women were as under:

i. In his earlier writings, he remarked that women are guardians of morality and sweet security of peace.

ii. Later as a result of his bitter experiences, his views changed. He stated that women should not possess individuality of their own. She should be subordinate to man. In the other words of Rousseau, 'A man seeks to serve, a woman seeks to please, the one needs knowledge, the other taste.'

iii. The ideal natural woman is modest, gentle, tolerant, submissive, amiable, chaste and charitable in her thoughts and actions.

iv. Girls have to be kept under more restraint and should be taught to be obedient and industrious.

So the *principles of education of women* were the following:

- The aim of educating women is to make her a perfect housewife with the ability to please man, and suffer and bear wrongs of her husband without complaint.
- The curriculum should comprise of —

  Physical education to develop her physical charm and develop healthy children,

  Domestic subjects to please her husband and look after the home, and Ethics and religion to make her god-fearing, and inculcate the values of sympathy and kindness. Method of teaching is teaching women to be busy.
- Discipline should be strict and not give her any freedom.

CONTRIBUTION TO EDUCATION

In the words of R.H.Duck, *"Rousseau did in the world of ideas what French Revolution afterwards did in the world of politics, he made a clean sweep and endeavoured to start afresh"*.

He opened new vistas for future educators. He advocated three important tendencies in Education — *Psychological tendency, Sociological tendency and Scientific tendency.*

i. Psychological tendency

As a preamble to the later psychologisation of education, the psychological principles emphasised by Rousseau were the following:

- Individual differences — Every individual has his own qualities. He replaced curriculum-centred education by child-centred education.
- Developmental stages was the focus of the selections of aims of education and the content of education.
- Natural endowments of the child — The educator should base the planning of the educational programme on the natural endowments of the child.
- Education by judgement and reason — The child should be given full freedom to form his own judgement.

ii. Sociological tendency

The foundations of sociological tendency were based on the principle that education should prepare the individual to live in society and develop in the individual the values of sympathy , co-operation, working together and benevolence.

iii. Scientific tendency

The scientific tendencies emphasised were as follows:

- Scientific approach by enabling the child to understand the why and wherefore of knowledge. He should be given the freedom to observe nature.
- Heuristic method — Rousseau recommended this method wherein the child is placed in the position of a discoverer.

iv. The other revolutionary ideas that he contributed were:

- the concept that education is organic growth. It is development from within.
- assertion that the child is a positive factor in education. Children should be considered as children before they are adults.

The methods of teaching advocated were *activity method, heuristic method, education through concrete things.*

He recommended *free discipline which will ensure the maximum development of the child.*

The contribution of Rousseau attracted great educationists of the world.

RELEVANCE TO PRESENT CONTEXT

Analysing the educational ideas of Rousseau and viewing the principles from the point of view of today's education and education for the future, the following observations may be made.

The importance given by him to the natural surroundings and inculcation of the love for Nature embodies the basic principles of Environmental Education and conservation of natural resources. Improvement of the quality of life which is suggested by Rousseau is quite applicable even today though the detailed concept of improvement may not be identically same. Improvement of quality of life according to him does not mean greater sophistication but a more natural life.

The psychological principles emphasised by Rousseau are applicable and useful when planning Human Resource Development for diversification of courses and Vocational Education.

The methods suggested by Rousseau are valuable in planning. Science Education for developing scientific humanism. He emphasises experimentation, creativity and a spirit of inquiry. The principles form the basis of the techniques of teaching.

His views on the rights of children are in co-ordination with the views of educationists and organisations like the UNICEF, CRY, which are trying to protect the rights of children by fighting against child abuse, exploitation of children, child labour.

The social values discussed by Rousseau reflect the process of socialisation and social skills and social values that we endeavour to promote. In his concept of social relations to be developed in the adolescent stage, he has given the basic principles of social service and community education which are so essential in the present context for dealing with national problems of poverty and illiteracy. His concept of visits to places of work is also very relevant for developing the social values.

The concept of free discipline and education for women are not applicable today, as women today are participating actively in national development. They are occupying leading positions in every field. Provisions are being made for equality of sexes.

His slogan of *'Back to Nature'* is applicable for creating awareness, Health Education and Physical Education. It is praise worth to note that he has included subjects which are most relevant in today's situation like sex education and trade.

His educational ideas have ushered in a new era in education and provided motivation to educational thinkers of the future.

PLATO (428 BC-347 BC)

Plato, the father of Idealism evolved a theory based on the Doctrine of the soul. This was the first attempt in Philosophy to understand the psychical life.

Biographical Sketch

Family background and Education: Plato belonged to a very respectable and aristocratic family. Ariston, his father, was a skillful player. In Greece, Education was imparted through various games and music. Consequently, Plato's education was based on these principles. Plato was a sportsman of the first order. He had won many wrestling bouts. He studied Homer and other Greek literature. He had a great love for literature and politics. He remained a bachelor throughout his life.

Plato becomes the disciple of Socrates: Plato had a love and respect for Socrates. Plato was greatly influenced by his ideals and preached them. It is said that *"If Socrates created the song of philosophy, it was Plato who sang the tune"*.

Plato wrote compositions in dialogue form. These compositions reflect moral behaviour.

Plato acquires vast experiences by his travel to various countries: After the death of Socrates, Plato left Athens and wandered far and wide, in search of truth and knowledge. He lived for some years in Egypt. He was impressed by the system of education in Egypt.

In Italy, he studied the ideas of Pythagoras. In Sicily, he attended the court of King Dionysurs and acquired knowledge of administration. Engaged as he was in quest of knowledge and truth, Plato gained sufficient knowledge in literary, political and social fields.

Evolution of Fundamental Philosophical concepts: As a result of his rich and wide experiences in far off lands, he became an expert philosopher, politician and social reformer. He influenced politics, religion and education system. His major contribution to the world were a general theory of philosophy embodying (a) Theory of new form of Government, (b) A new social order, and (c) A well articulated system of education.

Setting up of a school: In order to test his educational ideas, he set up a school on Greek tradition in 386 B.C. at a place provided by his friends and disciples. He was engaged in the establishment and organisation of the school till the very end of his life. In this school, he provided for the teaching in mathematics, philosophy, education, sociology, politics and music.

Plato's works

Plato's philosophy was the subject-matter of his works which were as follows:

a. *Republic*	a treatise dealing with his views on justice, ideal state, education.
b. *Laws*	an old age compilation to clarify certain portions of Republic.
c. *Protagoras*	a treatise on Socratic doctrine of virtue.
d. *Symposium*	a treatise on concept of Platonic love for truth, beauty and goodness as differentiated from the popular sensuous love.
e. *Timoeus*	an allegorical exposite of the drama of creation.

GENERAL PHILOSOPHY OF LIFE

i. **Doctrine of the soul**: It is the central part of the system of Plato's philosophy. The *fundamental principles* of this doctrine are:

a. *Soul springs from the ideal world* which is manifest in its yearning for the beautiful and its effort to gain mastery over the physical part of nature.

b. *Soul of man is three-fold* — Man, Lion and a charioteer driving two horses, one of noble nature and the other of ignoble nature. The noble nature is constantly striving to mount to the heavenly region in quest of the images of divine beauty and wisdom which are proper to its nature. The ignoble nature is constantly dragging it down to earth. Soul is by itself indestructible and divine but becomes influenced by the physical world. The supreme soul is immortal and possesses a vitality which survives all change. *The supreme aim of the soul is to break the power of evil and attain freedom and goodness.*

ii. **Pythagorean doctrine of transmigration after death.**

iii. **Theory of knowledge**:

Types of knowledge

gained through senses (not permanent, unreal)	gained through opinions (useful in certain situations, not real and true, half-thought)	that which is innate (It is in the mind ormanent, reason. Consists of abstract ideas, independent of experi ence universal, unchangeable)

iv. **Reality**, according to Plato, the idealist persists and beauties never fade. In the field of reality, man lives in two worlds.

(a) *World of ideas* — It is the real world. It is away from worldly objects. It is eternal, spaceless, unbounded and unchangeable. It is true and genuine. The absolute ideas are entities in themselves. They are inter-related in a heavenly order. All worldly objects are created and modelled according to them. True reality is thought, therefore, it is spiritual.

(b) *World of senses and objects* — It is the material world. Everything is in space and time, everything is subject to change. Plato regards matter as source of evil and the cause of all imperfections. Beautiful things fade away but the concept of beauty remains.

v. **Man is the essence of the universe.** He is a combination of body and soul. Man's body and soul have to be developed to enable him to be perfect and lead a moral life. Body is made of physical components. It is the source of all evils. Body is unreal and transitory. Soul has three elements. They are as follows:

- *Instincts and appetites* — They are the first part of the soul. The centre of this element is the abdomen. It instigates or enhances desires, wishes and other activities of the body. This part is subject to decay and destruction. Therefore instincts, drives, urges and desires have to be curbed.

- *Will* is the second element. It resides in the heart. It is a source of encouragement for all activities. It inspires endurance, perseverance and tolerance.
- *Reason* has its centre in the mind. It is divine and not related to the body. It is indestructible and does not change. It resides in the divine power of God before birth. After birth its abode is the soul. Wisdom unfolds truth, beauty and goodness to the soul. The aim of man's life should be to realise this wisdom and be happy, delighted and contented. The aim of education should be to awaken the wisdom of man.

vi. **Mind is of two types.** They are as follows:

- *Empirical Mind* begins from the part and proceeds to the whole.
- *Rational Mind* begins from the whole and moves to the parts.
- The whole is superior to the parts.
- Ends are more important than the means.
- Mind can help in achieving bliss, supernatural and spiritual happiness and delight. Brain is the seat of the mind — the reason.

vii. **Values or the Good is the highest reality in the universe.** These virtues have their root in the psychological nature of man. Each element has its corresponding virtue. The values are the following:

- *Eternal values* — Truth, beauty, goodness.
- *Self control* — essential for character formation. It is important for appetite. Courage is the value of the heart. It is the fundamental virtue for individual and civic life. It should be active. Wisdom and reason should decide things at all times.
- *Justice* is the final virtue. It helps other faculties of the soul to carry on their proper function. It helps man to maintain an inter-relationship between the various elements of complex nature.

- The *moral and manners* of every citizen should be under drastic censorship. Moral habits should be inculcated in the youth with the help of a fixed and unchangeable system of training.

viii. **Body and material world are the source of evil** as material world is subject to decay and death, and body shares all the weaknesses of the material world, deprives the reason and is worse than a prison to the soul.

ix. **The State occupies the first place.** It is a divine agency with a divine function of realising the Good upon the earth. It has ethical ends and is absolutely supreme.

x. **Individual exists in the state.** Individual has many wants which cannot be satisfied by his own efforts. State is in a position to provide these wants. The individual, therefore, occupies the second place.

xi. **Family has individualized tendencies.** So it is not important. The family associations has no value in comparison with the State which is paramount. Breeding, nursing and training of children should be controlled by the State. Family life is to be permitted to the slaves only.

EDUCATIONAL PHILOSOPHY

Concept of Education

Education is the fairest thing that the best of men should have. Education is an essential function of a cosmic order. It leads to the pursuit of integrity, goodness and perfection.

Definition of Education

1. Education is a moral training and an attempt on the part of the older generation to pass on to the coming generation all the good habits, wisdom, moral values and qualities that have been acquired by the generation through experience.

2. Education is that training which is given by suitable habits to the first instincts of virtue in children, which lead you always to hate what you ought to hate, and love what you ought to love from the beginning of life to the end.

Aims and Functions of Education

The major function of Education as stated by Plato is "Education consists of giving to the body and the soul all the perfection of which they are capable." Further, on the basis of his philosophy of life, the aims, purpose and functions of education are as follows:

i. *Maintaining unity and solidarity of the State* by developing a team and co-operative spirit, and thereby a feeling of community life; providing a training by which the individual would submit himself to the authority of the state; sacrifice personal interests for the sake of the state and dedicate himself to the service of the state and society.

ii. *Developing an ideal citizenship* by inculcation of civic virtues and ideals of ideal citizenship in the youth by developing civic efficiency, inculcating the habits of temperance, courage and military skills.

iii. As it is knowledge acquired through reason that is true, permanent and eternal, the third aim of education has to be *to develop the rule of reason* in the youth so that appetites and desires do not have the upper hand.

iv. *Produce the love for Truth, Beauty and Goodness.*

v. *Harmonising the personality of the individual and thus produce a whole or unified man* by co-ordinating the body and mind, the life of habit and the life of reason, individual interests and interests of the state.

vi. *Producing self-governing individuals* — Education must be a substitute for state regimentation and innumerable laws.

vii. *By inculcation of manners and morals* — Education should make the school a humanising and socialising agency.

viii. *Provision of same type of education compulsorily* through state-controlled schools to ensure that no child is allowed to have his own will apart from that of the community.

FORM AND PROCESS OF EDUCATION

Forms of education are two-fold. They are:

- *Education for practical affairs* — This makes one efficient in daily activities and enables him to get knowledge of agriculture, trade or art. This education is mean and illiberal and of a low degree.

- *Education for service to the state* — This education is true and liberal. It makes man an ideal citizen. It enables him to fulfil his rights and duties as a citizen. In liberal education, fundamental virtues and rational virtues are developed.

The *process of education* involves the following:

- Value Education through music, discipline and military training.
- Conversion of life of senses to ideal reality by developing the rational faculty through the study of arithmetic.
- Compulsory intellectual training through principle of formal discipline in older students.
- Uniformity to produce the co-operative spirit required for the welfare of the state. The **eight rules** for carrying out this training are:

1. Moral environment
2. Censorship of morals and manners
3. Censorship of painting and sculpture
4. Elimination of ancient poetry and musical innovation
5. Excluding persons practising pantomime
6. Fixed games
7. Reverence for antiquity
8. Rituals of religion

CURRICULUM

According to the stages of development of life, he suggested a curriculum as follows:

Stage	*Curriculum*
Birth to 3 years (Infancy stage)	Proper nourishment and care. Safe development of the body. No teaching of subjects.
3 to 6 years (Nursery stage)	Plays, stories, fairy tales of virtuous thought, national stories.

6 to 13 years (Elementary stage) Seperate residence for boys and girls	Music, play and games, religion, morals, mathematics. Harmonising, controlling and co-ordinating movements of boys and girls Music is essential for development of mind and soul
13 to 16 years (Middle School Stage)	Instrumental Music, religion, poetry, arithmetic. Less or more time for music than the law allows should not be spent.
16 to 20 years (Gymnastic Stage)	Special training in games and gymnastics and military science, skill of riding, use of weapons, military training.
20 to 30 years (Higher stage)	Selection for a 10 year course of higher education. Higher Mathematics, geometry, astronomy science, philosophy. Philosophy, psychology, sociology, law, education.
30 to 35 years (Administrative Stage)	Promotion to superior cadre. Retirementat 50
50 onwards (Contemplative Stage)	Higher philosophy. Search of truth.

He viewed the practical and industrial arts with contempt as suitable only for slaves and as activities which deprived man of pleasure of real life. He recommended education for businessmen and administrators but was against education and training for slaves. He wanted that they should follow the traditional life and profession of the family. He recommended learning of domestic work by imitation for girls.

METHODS OF TEACHING

The methods suggested by him were:

- Pupil-centred method
- Play method

- Correlation
- Questioning Method
- Imitation

ROLE OF THE TEACHER

The teacher, i.e., the educator has the greatest importance. The educator is the torch bearer who leads man from darkness of the cave to the light. He is thus a guide.

DISCIPLINE

In the earlier stages, there should be no compulsion. Later on, discipline should evolve out of the inculcation of values and training.

EDUCATION OF WOMEN

Plato considered men and women as equal in the patronage of the state though women are weaker in strength. Both men and women should be taught music, dancing, gymnastics, military exercise, art of warfare and horsemanship.

CONTRIBUTION TO EDUCATION

Plato's ideas on education and his philosophy provided a basis for the later systems of education and the principles of education. His outstanding contributions to education were as follows:

- *Education system and the curriculum for the various stages* — This system reflects the philosophical, psychological and sociological foundations of education in its totality.
- *Idealistic concept of education* — Ethical values, idealism and character building was the nucleus of the entire theory of education.
- *Education at early stages without compulsion* — He emphasised education for enjoyment.
- *Suitable selection* — An individual should select what he is most suited for.
- *Equality of the sexes* — This principle of education he enunciated is characteristic of his foresight and insight. He remarked "Neither a woman as a woman or a man as a man has any special function but the gifts of nature are equally diffused in both the sexes."
- *Socialistic character of the scheme* — State is given an over-all control over education which may be valuable in *universalisation of education and education for all.*

- *Interblending of practice and theory* — The gradation of education and its linkage with the stages of development has a message for making education related to life and skill-oriented rather than theoretical and bookish.
- *Life of calmness and activity* — The quality of life, peace, harmony and the spiritual values of life leading to aesthetic enjoyment was emphasised.

RELEVANCE IN THE PRESENT CONTEXT

Plato's philosophy and his ideas on education provide food for thought and implementation for all educationists of today and even in the future, even though these ideas were visualised 2350 years ago.

The universal ideals of Truth, Beauty and Goodness bear the very essence of Aesthetics, Arts, Culture and the enrichment of the quality of life bereft of all its distortions and perversions. These universal values are concurrent with the universal values of our ancient philosophers and our culture, namely, Satyam, Shivam, Sundaram. This principle, advocated by Plato, can be gainfully applied in Environmental Education. Value Education and Character Formation is the need of the hour when materialism is superseding the higher values of life and leading to tensions of a diverse nature.

Aesthetic Education and Mental Discipline played a dominant role in his system of education. Today, aesthetic education and mental discipline are of vital importance.

Reason gave rise to permanent reality according to Plato. Today rational outlook has a great value in developing the higher faculties of the mind.

Participation of women in National Development and equality of the sexes and women's education is the main thrust of 'Education for All'. So Plato's emphasis on education of women is a pace-setter for the empowerment of women which is stressed upon today.

The principles of Plato's ideas which are not in keeping with the present context are:

- neglect of education for the labouring class.
  the individual and catering to individual differences are totally neglected whereas in today's system, developing the individual as an integral part of Human Resource Development is afforded priority.

- there is no place for the family whereas in the present context, the family plays a dominant role in the development of the child.
- Plato over-emphasises the commitment of the individual to the state.

7

ROLE OF THE TEACHER IN A CHANGING INDIAN SOCIETY

- *Changing times and complex roles*
- *Expectation of the pupils, the heads of the institutions, the parents, the society and the teachers*
- *Various roles played by the teacher*
- *Professional Ethics*
- *Demands of Political Ideologies*
- *Role of the teacher in achieving various goals*

ROLE OF THE TEACHER IN A CHANGING INDIAN SOCIETY

"The function of the teacher is of vital importance.He must be a committed man, committed to faith in the future of man, in the future of humanity, in the future of this country and the world. He must work with this implicit confidence in the power of humanity, in the recuperative power which it has and by which it can cleanse and purify itself.Unless he has faith in that he will never be able to advance higher."

- Dr Sarvapalli Radhakrishnan
(speeches and writings, 1965, p.20)

In ancient times, the teacher or the Guru was highly esteemed in society. He was great in learning.He was a reservoir of knowledge and was totally devoted to the cause of teaching with a missionary zeal and spirit of self-sacrifice. The teachers were considered to be useful members of society. It was, therefore, laid down that both the public and the state should help the learned and educational institutions by providing all the necessary financial resources.

The Guru was the spiritual and intellectual father of his students. The high esteem in which the Guru was held is indicated by the shloka which is commonly quoted.

Gurur Brahmaa Gurur Vishnuh
Gurur Devo Maheshvarah;
Gurureva param Brahma
tasmai Shree Gurave namah

The Guru is identified with all the deities of the Trinity. The function of the teacher was to lead the students from darkness of ignorance to light. He was the role model for his students. The spiritual salvation of the students depended upon the guidance of the Guru who was expected to help them to achieve excellence.The Guru was an embodiment of scholarship, modesty, morality and righteousness. He was god-fearing and pious. The teachers were the custodians of culture.

The Gurus of the ancient times influenced their students in every way as the students resided at the Ashram which had both the characteristics of a home and an educational institution.The teacher had few students to teach.So an intimate relationship was established between the teacher and the students.

Changing times and complex roles of the teacher

Changing times and changing political situations brought about rapid changes in the educational system.Educational institutions were established.Rapid developments in every field and ushering in of new technologies in the field of education brought about radical changes in the roles of the teacher, making teaching a complex and challenging activity.The factors responsible for the complexity and multi-faceted nature of the role of the teachers were the following:

- Knowledge explosion and radical changes in the content-area of all disciplines.
- New trends in techniques of teaching like programmed-learning, team-teaching, computer assisted instruction.
- Need for appropriate utilisation of the mass media.
- Problem of mass education and of large numbers in the class from varied family backgrounds and socio-economic groups.
- Increasing social expectations, changing social needs and complex social problems.
- Need to develop attitudes in adherence to the democratic, secular and socialist pattern of our government.
- Necessity of recognising the value of alternative strategies to Formal Education in tackling the problems of wastage and stagnation and the high rate of drop outs.

Thus the roles of the teachers underwent a transformation from that of imparting knowledge to developing the higher mental faculties of the child through a systematic stimulus variation and adoption of teaching methodology. The changes in the role of the teacher are explained in the following excerpts from the Report of the International Commission on Development of Education (1972).

The teacher's duty is less and less to inculcate knowledge and more and more to encourage thinking, his formal functions apart, he will have to become more and more an adviser, a partner to talk to, someone who helps seek out conflicting arguments rather than handing out ready-made truths.He will have to devote more time and energy to productive and creative activities, interaction, discussion, stimulation, understanding and encouragement.

Regarding the role of the teacher, the Commission on Development of Education states *"In general the teacher's role is changing in that authoritative delivery of knowledge is being supplemented by spending more time diagnosing the learner's needs, motivating and encouraging study, and, checking the knowledge required."*

The role of the teacher according to the Commonwealth Report (1974) is stated as follows:

"The teacher has a major role in educational development, whether he approaches his work actively or passively. He can influence development adversely by opposition, innovation or merely remaining mute in the face of a growing need of reform. On the other hand, he can participate actively as the initiator himself or an interpreter of the plans devised by others."

The role of the teacher according to the Education on the Move (1975) is stated as follows:

"The work of the teacher consists moreover, less and less in providing the student with knowledge, and more and more in helping him to organise himself, to organise by himself the flood of information he receives from the environment in order to make it his own knowledge readily available to him and enabling him to live and act."

All these excerpts indicate that the teacher is instrumental in developing the individual and contributing to educational development by his democratic approach, creative initiation and innovative practices.

So the duties of the teacher, the roles of the teacher and the professional ethics of the teacher have to go hand in hand and work in co-ordination towards the fulfilment of the expectations of the children, the parents, the institutional authorities and the nation.

Hence before we proceed to the discussion of the roles of the teacher, we discuss the expectations of the students, institutional authorities, parents and the nation.

Expectations of the Pupils

The qualities that pupils expect in their teachers are as follows:

- in-depth knowledge of the content
- ability to communicate, to understand, to relate, to satisfy the curiosity of pupils
- ability to discipline without curbing the freedom of the children and to be firm

- impartial judgement
- high moral character
- practising what s/he preaches and not having double standards
- friendliness with a sense of dignity, i.e. not trying for cheap popularity
- good personality
- emotionally stable
- sense of humour
- dedicated to teaching profession
- enthusiasm
- ability to inspire and motivate students
- intelligent and alert
- caring about students
- reasonably approachable
- ability to identify and develop talents of pupils and a sense of appreciation

In other words, as research studies indicate, students prefer teachers with dynamism, humaneness, depth of knowledge and capacity to inspire, stimulate, motivate, enlighten, enrich and enhance the faculties of the students.

Expectations of the heads of institutions

The heads of institutions are keen about the progress of the institution and its image in society and its status in comparison with other institutions of the same category. So the expectations of the heads of institutions are as follows:

- regularity and punctuality
- sincerity
- up-to-date knowledge of the subject
- teaching competency
- versatile abilities
- result-oriented approach without sacrificing the interest of achieving all-round development of the pupils

- ability to inspire, motivate and develop the thinking strategies and reasoning ability of the pupils
- good communicating, organising and managerial skills
- values of positive attitudes to work, co-operation, economic and social upliftment
- adherence to the principles and goals of the institution
- desire to work for the growth of the institution and for the prestige of the institution
- devotion to the task of teaching
- love for children
- sociable and amicable nature

On the whole, the heads of institutions expect disciplined behaviour, teaching proficiency, effective communication, good impact on the children and high sense of commitment and involvement.

Expectations of the parents

The parents are, to a great extent, the representatives of the community to which the school belongs. They are greatly concerned about the achievements of their children, their behaviour, their progress and their future. So the qualities they expect of the teacher are as follows:

- kindness
- patience
- ability to establish rapport
- understanding of the parents' concern
- maturity
- problem-solving ability
- consistency in behaviour
- respect for others and their view point
- diagnostic approach to children's problems
- positive approach
- ability to listen, interact and communicate effectively, i.e. effective management of public relations

Expectations of Society

Education produces the man-power and the human resources that the society needs for its economic, social and cultural development. The teacher moulds and shapes the raw material given by the society into the human resources for social upliftment. In a way, the industrial and vocational organisations are the consumers. Hence, the general tendency is to view the teacher as shouldering the responsibility for the individuals produced by the schools. Therefore, the expectations of society from the teachers are as follows:

- dissemination of up-to-date knowledge
- development of personality of pupils with a skill and competency-based approach, enabling them to prepare for and take up a vocation of their choice
- awareness of the needs, aspirations and culture of the society.
- understanding of the problems of society
- sense of social commitment
- humanistic approach to the socio-economic problems of children
- good rapport with the leaders, social organisations in the area and of a similar category
- excellence as a community educator

Expectations of the Teachers

Education can be effective and fruitful if there is a mutual co-operation between the interacting agencies.Therefore, the fulfilment of expectations have to be reciprocal and complementary. The expectations of the teachers are as follows:

- respect by pupils
- a congenial working environment at school
- job-security
- facilities for professional development and teacher resource enrichment
- an organisational climate of trust, freedom, impartial justice and mutual confidence among members

- co-operation and co-ordination of parents in developing the personality of the pupils with an understanding of the difficulties and problems of the teachers
- social status and dignity in society
- higher economic status to facilitate an improvement in quality of life through provision of better amenities

ROLES OF THE TEACHER

The views of the International Commissions, the roles of the teacher according to the various educational thinkers discussed in the previous chapter and the expectations of the factors involved in the process of education provide the basis for the discussion of the roles of the teachers. An understanding of the roles of the teachers will give a better perspective of the professional ethics of the teachers.

The roles of the teacher in the teaching-learning situation are as follows:

Co-learner: In a democratic set-up, the teacher is no more an authoritative custodian of knowledge transferring it to the pupils in the classroom. He has to play a participatory role by being a co-learner. Both the pupils and the teacher are learning from the experiences, by exchanging ideas and interacting.

Friend, philosopher and guide: The teacher-pupil relationship is a friendly relationship. By creating a congenial environment for establishing a rapport, the teacher gains the confidence of his pupils. With a maturity of thought and deep insight, the teacher guides the thoughts and actions of the pupils. The teacher's concern for his pupils are like those of a parent.

Director: In this role, the teacher directs the entire teaching-learning programme. She plans the educational programme keeping the objectives to be achieved in view. She implements the educational programme and provides relevant experiences with a variety, creating interest, thereby making it a memorable fruitful experience for the pupils.

Animator: When the technique adopted is a group discussion, the teacher initiates the discussion and puts life into it by animating the discussion. As animator, she motivates those unwilling participants to participate.

Motivator: Motivation is an important factor that promotes learning. The teacher adopts various strategies to motivate the pupils to overcome their inhibitions, participate whole heartedly in the learning situation, to interact freely with the teacher and other members of the group.

Facilitator: The critical element in performing this role is the personal relationship between the facilitator and the learner. This personal relationship depends upon the attitudinal qualities of the teacher or the facilitator, his genuineness, non-possessive, caring, his trust and respect and value for the individuality of the pupils, empathic understanding, sensitive and accurate listening. The steps to facilitate learning are as follows:

- setting the initial mood or climate
- clarifying the purposes of the individual members and of the group
- establishing the motivational force of the individuals and the group
- making the whole range of resources available including the teacher who is a flexible resource to be utilised by the group
- responding both to the intellectual aspect and emotional attitudes of the individuals and the group
- establishing an acceptant climate
- becoming a participant as one of the group

Administrator: In this role, the teacher controls the entire learning situation and maintains discipline, while taking care to see that all members of the group get adequate freedom of thought and expression. S/he is the organiser of the entire learning activity.

Co-ordinator: The teacher co-ordinates all the experiences and ideas of all the members of the group.

Leader: In a democratic setting, the teacher leads the entire group through a variety of learning experiences accepting ideas, encouraging each individual to react freely, and formulate ideas, leading to a consensus.

Evaluator: The unbiased opinion of the teacher along with his\her power judgement and critical awareness are the essential requisites of this role. The teacher evaluates the outcome of the learning programme not as an end in itself but to analyse the merits and demerits and improve upon it.

Researcher: The teacher can be effective only if his\her teaching is supplemented by constant research. These researches are more of the nature of Action Researches and most often experimental.

The teacher's work does not end with the classroom but lies even outside the classroom. According to Mahatma Gandhi, *"Unless teachers are prepared to give all their time outside the classroom to their students, not much can be done.Let them fashion their hearts rather than their brains"*. Though it may not be practicable for the teachers to give all their time to the students, in the present context, the teachers can achieve a lot by awakening their curiosity, enriching their perception and elevating their minds.

The teacher is an integral part of the community. So the main roles of the teacher in the community are:

Reformer: By developing desirable social attitudes, the teacher can create awareness in the community about the social evils and social problems and bring about social reforms.

Community Educator: The teacher utilises his expertise and skills to pool the available resources, mobilise them and achieve community development through community education.

A. PROFESSIONAL ETHICS

The teacher is the pivot of the man-making and nation building process. The teacher is the agent of social change and a catalyst. If a teacher has to fulfil these major responsibilities with excellence, professional ethics and a code of conduct is essential. The impression that a teacher makes on his pupils is an ever-lasting and sometimes supercedes all other influences. Often it is responsible for the child's affinity or aversion to the school environment and even education itself. In fact, to the very young children the teacher is like God and the words, actions and behaviour of the teacher is a model for emulation. Contrarily, the dislike of a teacher may lead to dislike of the subject taught by her. Sometimes, the cause of indiscipline is the teacher's incompetency. The following statements by Mahatma Gandhi substantiate the need for a teacher to have a strong moral character.

"The politician may succeed in his purpose even though he lacks character, but a people's teacher cannot do without character. If he lacks, he will be like salt without its savour."

- True Education, (p.161)

"I have found that boys imbibe more from the teachers' own lives than they do from the books that they read to them or the lectures that they deliver to them with their lips."

- To students (p.15)

Hence it is the teacher's philosophy, views and behaviour that can help the students to develop a philosophy of life, besides the endeavours to inculcate values and culture.

The fundamental principle of the professional ethics of the teacher may be classified into:

- Philosophical principles
- Psychological principles
- Sociological principles

PHILOSOPHICAL PRINCIPLES

Positive thinking

In order to overcome the setbacks and to achieve success in life, one has to develop positive attitude to life and think positively. If the teacher has to develop the positive attitude in the pupils, the teacher has to have a positive attitude to the day to day classroom problems. The teacher must have a positive outlook in correcting the mistakes of the pupils and avoid negative remarks.Similarly, there may be limitations or draw-backs in the institution and her colleagues. These can be tackled with a positive approach. Thus, the social interaction and relationships will be one of concord leading to a harmonious smooth functioning of the institution. The principle of harmo-nious co-existence and the value of co-operation can be inculcated in the pupils.

Life-long learning

This principle is emphasised by Rabindranath Tagore in the following words.

"A teacher can never truly teach unless he is still learning himself. A lamp can never light another lamp unless it continues to burn its own flame."

A teacher has to cope up with the developments in the modern world and with the explosion of knowledge. So in the absence of an interest in learning, she will be imparting outdated information. Besides, when the present day children are exposed to a variety of sources of latest information, the teacher will find herself in an embarrassing situation and lose her confidence. The teacher should derive pleasure from life-long learning as every experience in life provides opportunity to learn.

Aesthetic sense

Love for children makes a teacher enjoy her work. It is the pleasure of being with children that makes her forget her own problems and worries. If she views children as beautiful creations which are to be developed with love and care, then teaching becomes a performing art capable of providing aesthetic experience through creativity by organising the learning experiences which provide moments for both the teacher and the pupils to enjoy. Unfortunately, with the pressures of large numbers in the class and the rigid courses and examinations, the present day teachers' overburdened schedule, the aesthetic pleasure of teaching becomes an unfulfilled dream.

Professional integrity

A teacher is deeply involved in nurturing the young minds of the citizens of tomorrow. So the teacher has a great responsibility in arousing the curiosity of children and satisfying their curiosity. The children ask a number of questions when their curiosity is awakened and the teacher is faced with the problem of answering these questions. The teacher's professional integrity lies (i) in the sincerity with which she answers the questions, (ii) the perfection with which she prepares and plans her teaching, (iii) the dedication with which she performs her duties, (iv) the involvement with which she undertakes responsibilities without following the principle - *This is not my job, why should I do it?* , (v) the fairness and impartial nature of the justice meted out to her pupils, (vi) the manner in which she analyses her own mistakes and compensates for them, and finally (vii) the open-mindedness with which she recognises and appreciates the contribution made by her colleagues and others in her successes and outstanding achievements. The professional integrity of the teacher is manifest in her behaviour and social relationships. The observation of the pupils, and their interpretation form the image of the teacher. Besides the priority she gives to the institutional interests, the welfare of her pupils and her own selfish interest is another determinant of her professional integrity. For example, teachers who fail students to compel them to take private tuitions from them and those teachers who leak out the question paper to get good results have no professional integrity and are unfit to be teachers.

Moral character

Character building and inculcation of values is one of the fundamental aims of education. In the present days when crime and violence is prevalent in society and forms an integral part of the themes of films and media presentations, value-oriented education encounters a number of problems. However, this vital task cannot be neglected.Therefore, it is very essential that the teacher provides a concrete example by her own principles and behaviour. According to the Education Commission (1964-1966), *"Of all the different factors which influence the quality of education and its contribution to national development, the quality, competence and character of teachers are undoubtedly the most significant."*

Education Commission 1964-66
3.01 p.46

Thus, it may be stated that teachers with a disciplined and enlightened mind, a sound philosophy of life, a virtuous character, and vast experience are valuable assets to the nation. They can successfully build a learning society with a wealth of human resources and a strong national character.

PSYCHOLOGICAL PRINCIPLES

Personality of the teacher

The way a teacher presents herself physically and intellectually, her demeanour, her manners, her handwriting, her aesthetic sense, - all these aspects have a long lasting effect on the personalities of the pupils. For example, a teacher who has a polite way of talking influences the pupils as they unconsciously imbibe it. A teacher who is clumsy in her chalkboard work unintentionally imparts the same untidiness to the pupils. Sometimes, the mannerisms of the teachers are imitated by the children. It is a well known fact that children learn by imitation. So a teacher has to be scrupulous about the personality traits that she projects, avoid mannerisms, and practise what she preaches. Again, as stated earlier, what she says, what she does and the way she behaves, have a greater impact on the pupils than all the dos and donts that she may list. A teacher's integrated and balanced personality, her mental equilibrium, her management skills and her principles - all these have a dominant role in developing the personalities of the pupils.

Teacher's role in the development of personality

The interactions, self-concept, perception of roles and perception of others - all these are some of the major concerns of personality development. The teacher has to recognise the fact that the children come to the school with personalities influenced by various forces like the inherited traits, the family background, the socio-economic status, and the cultural background. The teacher plays an important role in the development of healthy, stable, well-integrated balanced personalities. At the same time, she cannot fail to take cognisance of the influence of external forces, both desirable and undesirable, which are reinforcing or undoing the teacher's influence.

Therefore the teacher has to achieve the goal of developing healthy, stable, integrated personalities by adopting these strategies:

- Providing a relaxed, stimulating environment in the classroom with full scope for freedom of expression, free from fear and conveying the teacher's love for them.
- Setting good example, and avoiding double standards saying one thing and doing another.

As stated by Mahatma Gandhi, *"Woe to the teacher who teaches one thing with the lips and carries another in the heart"*.

- M. K. Gandhi

(True Education p.161)

A teacher who has double standards creates value conflicts in her pupils which is harmful to the development of personality.

Teacher as Motivator

Motivation accelerates the rate of learning and its quality. The teacher has to adopt various techniques to fulfil the physical, emotional and cognitive needs of the students. By providing a comfortable physical environment, she satisfies the physical needs; by treating the pupils with respect and love, she satisfies the emotional needs of self-esteem, and by providing stimulating tasks like games, puzzles, she fulfils the pupils need to achieve.

The teacher should be creative and innovative in selecting the learning experiences. Proper selection of learning experiences requires commitment and involvement on the part of the teacher.

Teacher as counsellor

Children encounter many problems and challenging situations in the process of development. There are many decisions to be taken. At such moments, it is the teacher who can provide the necessary guidance and counselling. The teacher cannot perform this role effectively unless she has a thorough understanding of the capacities of her pupils and a deep concern for their future.

Besides, she must be well-equipped with the relevant information to suggest the proper course of action. In case of children with learning disabilities or those who are under achievers, she must be in a position to diagnose the problem and suggest the proper remedial measure. She may, at times, have to counsel the parents when she feels that a change in the parents' attitude is necessary. The teacher has primarily to understand the problem, analyse it, collect all the necessary information and then make her suggestions tactfully, without damaging the personality of the pupil or the parents. A humanistic approach, with kindness, warmth and empathy is necessary. She has to communicate effectively, give a patient listening to other's viewpoints and then convey her ideas.

SOCIOLOGICAL PRINCIPLES

A teacher cannot be isolated from society. She is a member of society and has developed in society. She is involved in the task of preparing the future citizens and developing human resources.

The main roles of the teacher are those pertaining to social development through social change and in building a healthy democratic learning society.

The prime requisite for playing this role effectively is her interest in society and her social and cultural awareness. It is essential for her to have an idea of the social structure, changing family patterns, social needs ad the existing social environment. Primarily, this understanding will provide the basis for her to understand some of the behaviour problems of her pupils arising out of their home and social environment.

To sum up, the professional ethics of a teacher comprise of the following qualities in the teacher.

- Desire to enrich knowledge and apply it to practical life-situations
- Positive approach to the challenges of teaching
- A thorough understanding of psychological principles and their application in teaching
- Humanistic approach in tackling discipline and behaviour problems
- Commitment to issues of national development

Education in an emerging Indian Society has to achieve the major goals of National Development accomplishing the tasks of developing an infra-structure for education for all through -

- Universalisation of Elementary Education
- Early Childhood Care and Education
- Modernisation
- Promoting National Integration and International Understanding
- Developing democratic values of Secularism, Social Justice
- Creating awareness essential for tackling social and national problems and for building a democratic society through attitudinal change through

  Population Education

  Environment Education Value-oriented Education and Awareness Raising Programmes

B. DEMANDS OF POLITICAL IDEOLOGIES

When considering the demands of political ideologies, it is essential to proceed step by step in the following manner:

- The preamble to our Indian Constitution and the concepts for which youth of the country has to be educated

- Constitutional Provisions pertaining to education
- Problems of National Development
- Education and National Development (Kothari Commission and National Policy of Education (1986))
- Roles of the teachers with regard to each goal

Preamble to the Indian Constitution and the concept for which the youth of the country has to be educated

The constitution of a country clearly reflects the political ideology in a practical down-to-earth form. It contains the objectives which the people of the country are committed and the ideals embodied in it which regulate their life and conduct.

The political ideologies involved in it are clearly stated in the first preamble to the constitution which are as follows:

'We, the people of India having solemnly resolved to constitute India into a Sovereign Socialist Secular Democratic Republic and to secure to all its citizens -

Justice, social, economic and political

Liberty of thought, expression, belief, faith and worship

Equality of status and of opportunity, and to promote among them all Fraternity, assuring the dignity of the individual and the unity and integrity of the nation.

Thus the political ideologies evolving out of the constitution are Socialism, Secularism and Democracy. The values to be promoted are the democratic values of Liberty, Equality of status and opportunities, Fraternity and Unity. It is further stated that the youth of the country should be educated for the democratic and socialist concept of social and economic order.

Constitutional provisions relating to Education

The constitutional provisions relating to education are as follows:

- Freedom to promote any religion
- Freedom of religious worship
- Protection of interests of minorities
- Provision for Free and Compulsory Education

- Promotion of educational and economic interests of scheduled castes (SC), scheduled tribes (ST) and other weaker sections
- Language of representation of grievance
- Facilities for instruction in Mother Tongue at Primary stage
- Directive of development of Hindi language
- Facilities for Higher Education and Research
- Participation in International Conferences, Associations and other bodies and implementing the recommendation

Problems of National Development

The problems of National Development encountered by the Government and that had to be tackled are the following:

- Increasing per capita income
- Improving the quality of life
- Modernising society
- Promoting emotional and national integration
- Raising adult literacy rate
- Population control
- Environment protection and conservation of resources
- Developing democratic, secular and social values
- Bringing out a synthesis between moral and scientific values

In the process of tackling these problems, education has a prominent role to play by providing the necessary facilities, planning and restructuring education with a view to achieving these objectives by creating awareness, and developing moral and social values. Commissions were appointed from time to time to evolve relevant strategies and define the role of the teachers in achieving national development.

Recommendations of the Commissions

The report of the Education Commission (1964-66) was significantly named as *Education and National Development.*

The intimate relationship between educational reconstruction and national development is given in the following excerpts from the report:

i. If the pace of national development is to be accelerated, there is need for a well-defined, bold and imaginative educational policy, and for determined and vigorous action to vitalise, improve and expand education.

ii. Education cannot be considered in isolation or planned in a vacuum. It has to be used as a powerful instrument of social, economic and political change and will therefore have to be related to the long-term national aspirations and the programmes of national development on which the country is engaged and the difficult short-term problems it is called upon to face.

iii. In a world based on science and technology, it is education that determines the level of prosperity, welfare and security of the people. On the quality and number of the persons coming out of our schools and colleges will depend our success in the great enterprise of national reconstruction whose principal objective is to raise the standard of living of our people.

The National Commission on Teacher I for School Teachers (1983-85) entitled its report as *The Teacher and Society*. The Commission stated the nation must unreserved commit itself to the welfare of the teacher and also to the raising of its status in society. The teacher in turn, is expected to dedicate himself to his duties and improvement of his professional competence and career.

The National goals are derived from the vision and ideals of the people and are consistent with those enshrined in the Constitution. The four national goals that have to be given top priority for the well-being of our people are:

i. A united secular India

ii. A modern nation

iii. A productive people

iv. A humane and caring society

According to National Policy on Education (1986) *"The country has reached a stage in its economic and technical development when a major effort has to be made to derive the maximum benefits from the assets already created and to ensure that the fruits of change reach all sections. Education is the highway to that goal.*

Human Resource Development is a man-making process. The teacher will have to identify the capacities and talents of the pupils and provide a variety of experiences to develop the personalities of the pupils. The teacher has to be creative and innovative in the experiences s\he provides.

The teacher has to provide a free environment in the classroom where the students are motivated to participate freely in the learning activity. The pupils should be encouraged so that they enjoy the activity.

Democratic methods

The techniques of teaching adopted by teachers should be democratic. They should develop the thinking and reasoning abilities of the pupils. The learning experiences and the activities conducted should be selected with a view to promoting the critical awareness of the pupils. Teachers should not impose their views on the pupils but afford full scope for the pupils to use their discretion.

Modernisation

Teachers must be open-minded and research-oriented and must conduct various experiments.

Teachers must emphasise the importance of critical awareness in adapting to social and cultural change. Scientific temper and rational outlook should be promoted.

They should adopt techniques which would arouse curiosity among the pupils. They should develop analytical and interpretative skills among the pupils.

Social Awareness

A humane and caring society can be developed by developing a sense of commitment to the society and the nation. The pupils should be made aware of the national problems like poverty, population explosion, environmental degradation. They should be made conscious of their responsibilities as citizens towards the tackling of these problems. Co-curricular and social service activities should aim at maximising social interaction, enhancing social relationships and fostering the values of co-operation, team spirit and co-existence.

Thus, the teachers play important roles in a democracy by developing the personalities of the pupils, inculcating democratic values and developing a national character, utilising educational technology gainfully to promote scientific attitude.

ROLE OF TEACHERS IN EQUALITY

The classroom is a miniature society where children belong to different family, social and cultural backgrounds. As a result, the pupils differ greatly in their abilities, talents and aptitudes. The children may belong to different socio-economic strata of society.

In a democratic society, it is essential that equal opportunities are provided for the minorities, scheduled castes, scheduled tribes, economically backward, handicapped and the girl-child.

The prime task of the teacher is to make himself/herself acquainted with the constitutional provisions and the facilities provided for each of these categories.

As a result, s/he must be careful to avoid making any negative remarks that would hurt the feelings of any of the categories.

Teachers should see that all are treated equally without any discrimination. Equal opportunities should be provided to all the categories of students to participate in the curricular andco-curricular activities.

Teachers should take precautions to identify complexes and remedy them with a positive approach.

Every pupil should be made to feel that the entire class is a family and every member should have equal opportunities for development. Wherever it is possible, they should help one another to overcome limitations and progress.

Teachers can effectively use group dynamics to achieve equality.

Activities that promote social interaction go a long way in reducing social distances. Scouts, guides, camps enable the pupils to understand that all children are equal and need to be treated with love, affection and understanding, irrespective of their socio-economic status and cultural background.

The National Policy on Education (1986) emphasises equality of opportunities to minorities, socially and economically disadvantaged, handicapped and women.In view of this, the teachers have a dominant role in creating the appropriate environment to promote equal opportunities. The pre-requisites of the appropriate environment are:

- a positive attitude on the part of the teacher emulated by the pupils, and
- a caring concern and empathy towards the problems of thedisadvantaged.

Teachers must play the roles of therapists by analysing the problems diagnostically and adopting therapeutic measures.

In the case of the handicapped who are being integrated into normal schools, the teacher has to be alert in understanding the difficulties of the child, the problems in communicating and interacting with other children in the class. The teacher has to create confidence in the child and motivate the child to develop a positive attitude. Besides, the teacher has to educate the other children in the class to be sensitive to the problems of the other children, who are disadvantaged or handicapped and help them. without creating a feeling of dependence or inferiority. The teacher has, therefore, to be a philosopher and social engineer. Teachers have to make the pupils realise that all human beings are equal. Every human being has equal rights. Every limitation or handicap is compensated by the gift of some special ability.For example, the blind are gifted with minute sense of hearing. S/he has to develop an appreciation among the pupils for the special talents of these children for outstanding achievers among the disadvantaged and handicapped.

Teachers can organise visits to special institutions, rural areas, slums and rehabilitation centres. Such visits will promote the democratic value of equality among the pupils. Besides, they will also realise their responsibilities in promotion of equality. They will realise that disadvantage is not a crime. It is not a cause for denial or discrimination. It calls for co-ordinated peoples' action to rehabilitate, empower and develop.

Today's pupils i.e. the girls and boys studying in the secondary schools are the men and women of tomorrow's society. The positive attitudes towards the equality of the sexes has to be developed in them by examples and by creating an awareness of the problems encountered by women and the need for a change in social attitudes

Thus, teachers can play a vital role in the promotion of equality and contribute to the building of a harmonious democratic society.

ROLE OF TEACHERS IN SOCIAL JUSTICE

Social Justice is a practical implementation of Equality. Social Justice implies the treatment meted out to people from various sections of society. Social justice evolves from the principle "*All human beings are equal in the eyes of the law.*" This means that there is no disparity in the judgement given between one group and another. The main objectives of social justice is to bridge the gap between urban and rural communities, rich and poor, educated and illiterate or uneducated. For example an outstanding deed is recognised and rewarded irrespective of any distinctions of the section of Society to which s/he belongs. Correspondingly a criminal is sentenced to punishment according to the penal code without any discrimination whatsoever.

The fundamental issues of Social Justice are the following:

Fighting against exploitation in various forms such as —

- child abuse and child labour.
- sexual harassmentand victimisation of women.
- iii-treatment and differentiation of male and female children.
- inequality of payment for labour i.e. paying women labourers less than the men labourers for the same job.
- depriving deserving candidates of their education or career without any valid reason.
- denial of legal rights and basic necessities of life for material gains of one individual.
- collecting large amounts as donations for rendering normal regular services.

While these are the factors where Social Justice has to adopt measures to eradicate injustice, Social justice has to find out means to tackle the problems of poverty, illiteracy, unemployment and under-employment.

The features of the National Policy on Education (1986) have been envisaged, bearing in mind the aspects of Social Justice leading to National Development.

The salient feature of the National Policy on Education emphasising Social Justice are the following:

- National system of Education to provide access to Education of a comparable quality to all students, tohave a common educational structure with national curricular framework having a common core.
- Equality of opportunity of education not only in access but also in the conditions for success. Awareness of the inherent quality of all will be created through the core curriculum. Removal of the prejudices and complexes transmitted through the social environment and by accident of birth.
- Minimum levels of learning will be laid down for every stage. Steps will be taken to foster among students an undertaking of the diverse cultural and social system of the people living in different parts of the country.
- Universalisation of Elementary Education
- Early Childhood Care and Educations
- Promotion of Women Education
- Vocationalisation of Education
- Examination reforms to rectify the inequalities between the priviieged who have facilities for special coaching, special learning materials and the under privileged who have no such facilities.

The features of the National Policy on Education (1986) will have no value unless they are implemented with an understanding of the significance and with the determination to achieve the national goal of social justice. So action-oriented approach will have to be coordinated with effective down to earth planning. Thus the role of teachers assumes an ever widening dimension.

The characteristic features of the role of the teacher in social justice are the following:

Behaviour and attitude of the teacher

The teacher promotes social justice or hampers it, (i)when she selects children for participation in the school activities (ii) when she rewards children or punishes them for their performance or behaviour (iii) when she evaluates their performance. In all these situations, the teacher has to be impartial and fair. The reaction of the teacher has to be commensurate with the deed of the child and not guided by preferences, prejudices and biases. The reward or punishment should not differ from one child to another according to the whims of the teacher. Evaluation should be constructive and reformative and not damage the personality of the child. The teacher should avoid making deciding statements about the family or cultural background of the child.

Removing misconceptions or wrong notions

It is commonly observed that pupils from the socially and economically backward classes reflect the notions of their parents that justice can be sought only by the rich as one has to pay heavily for it. Besides, their complaints will not be attended to as they are poor. Harassment and intimidation has to be quietly endured because of their low social status. The teacher has to build up their confidence and make them understand that they should fight against exploitation and injustice. The teacher has to create awareness among the weaker sections about their rights and freedom that they are entitled to. The teacher can invoke legal practitioners and request them toorient the pupils regarding their legal rights. Social workers who are associated with voluntary organisations can be invited to furnish information about the activities of the voluntary organisations and the assistance provided by them for redressal of grievances of injustice violation of human rights. Similarly programmes for Consumer Awareness can be organised. Such programmes can enable the pupils to become aware of their rights as consumers and also to acquire information about Consumer Grievance Redressal Services. Thus the teacher can help to promote social justice by furnishing information regarding various aspects of human rights and justice.

ROLE OF TEACHERS IN UNIVERSALISATION OF ELEMENTARY EDUCATION

Every individual has a right to education, right to work, freedom to express his ideas. It is incumbent on programmes of National Development to assure the satisfaction of minimum needs of the individual - food, shelter, clothing and decent standard of living. Enabling individuals to acquire this through education is a fundamental requisite of sustainable development. Providing for minimum levels of Education is vital requisite of Social Justice. Hence universalisation of Elementary Education and provision for Early Childhood Care and Education are important elements of Social Justice. The prime task of the teacher is to create an awareness regarding the importance of education and about the facilities available in the form of freeships, scholarships, books and uniforms. The teachers can provide the necessary parental education for early childhood care. Teachers can associate themselves with the ECCE programme and cooperate by guiding those involved in the ECCE programme. While the UEF and ECCE programmes ensure enrolment, retention of the children enrolled till the completion of school education is a major problem. So the teacher has to create a stimulating motivating environment in the class so that the children enjoy the learning activity. The teacher has to make special efforts to establish rapport with the children and remove their fear of the teacher and the school atmosphere. Every care has to be taken to see that the children do not feel that the studies are beyond their capacity. The teacher should have personal contact with the pupils and guide them to solve their difficulties. Teachers can encourage the school pupils to participate in Literacy programmes by making the pupil realise their social responsibilities and commitment to national problems.

Thus teachers can enkindle the spirit of Social Justice in their pupils by bringing about a social awakening and arousing their indignation to violation of human rights and social injustice.

ROLE OF TEACHERS IN SOCIAL AND NATIONAL INTEGRATION AND INTERNATIONAL UNDERSTANDING

National Integration means a feeling among people to share common objectives, purpose or ideals and give them high place over smaller or sectional loyalties. It is the feeling of oneness which may transcend all group or cultural differences and synthesize the different castes, linguistic communities emotionally into a common whole.

Among the four national goals mentioned by National Policy on Teachers *A United Secular India is one of the major goals.*

The goal of National Integration is expressed in many ways in the Vedas in prayer.

"Let all be happy, let all be healthy,

Let all be noble, let none have sorrow and the world is a family

Now the concept has widened its dimensions and we talk in terms of World Family and a World Culture.

Education has a vital role to play in strengthening emotional and national integration. It should develop all aspects of students' personality. It should broaden the outlook and foster a feeling of oneness and nationalism. It should develop a spirit of sacrifice and tolerance so that narrow interests of the group are submerged in the large interests of the nation and the world.

In this task of education, *the teachers have to play dominant roles* which are as follows:

Teachers have to observe certain norms in their own behaviour. While teaching social studies and other school subjects, they should avoid making statements indicating their personal prejudices. Sweeping generalisations about the characteristics of particular communities or negative remarks should be avoided. Every student should be viewed as an individual human being and an Indian and not as a Hindu, Muslim, Christian, etc.

Emphasis should be laid on the common aspects of all religions and cultures.

Teachers should organise objective-oriented co-curricular activities like celebration of religious and national festivals, sports, educational visits, excursions, tours and camps.

Teachers can participate in activities for promotion of spirit of Unity and National Integration like community singing and cultural programmes organised by various bodies and committees. They can organise similar programmes in the schools.

Teachers must encourage hobby activities like stamp collection, coin collection, cultural exchange programmes, scout's camps and girl-guides. Such activities will promote community life and the spirit of oneness.

Essay competitions, debates, elocution competitions and various competitions can be organised on themes pertaining to National Integration.

Projects on various nations and states can be organised so that the pupils collect maximum information on other states and nations with curiosity and interest. Talks by people from other countries can be arranged to facilitate interaction and exchange of ideas.

In all these activities, teachers have to be enthusiastic themselves, provide all the reference material and guide the pupils in every stage of the project.

Thus, teachers have to make proper use of the common core of the various subjects to promote values such as India's common cultural heritage, egalitarianism, democracy, secularism, equality of the sexes, protection of the environment and removal of social barriers. Teachers' attitudes play an important part in developing the attitudes of the pupils to the world as a beautiful place with diverse peoples, diverse cultures, strives unitedly to build a better world. Teachers should teach pupils the value of inter-dependence, peaceful co-existence and co-operation. They should encourage the pupils to read newspapers and magazines to acquire the latest information. Teachers should orient the pupils regarding the achievements of outstanding scientists, writers, philosophers of the world and their endeavours to make the world a better place.

The concept of International Understanding could be infused through the school subjects effectively if the teacher has the proper insight, proper attitude and skills of teaching.

ROLE OF TEACHERS IN SECULARISM

Secularism implies that there is no imposition of religious or sectarian practices and observances under the law of the country. Every group or individual has complete right to choose and practise whichever faith or creed s/he desires. No particular faith or creed is particularly encouraged by government. Dr.B.R.Ambedkar stated, *"Secular state is one in which the Government would not interfere by imposing anyone religion on its people"*. Dr. Rajendra Prasad, First President of Free India stated, "*Secularism does not mean lack of religion or spiritual values. Freedom is granted to practise and preach whatever faith, religion and beliefs they want to. All religions are of equal value in the eyes of the state. No preference is to be given by the Government to anyone.*"

ROLE OF THE TEACHERS

Teachers should not show any special preference or prejudice to any religion, faith or creed in his/her statements or actions. Teachers should be careful when they interpret historical events or discuss the achievements of historical personalities.

Fostering spirit of tolerance

The spirit of tolerance should be inculcated in the pupils by displaying the spirit of tolerance when discussing controversial issues.

Respect for all religions

Teachers can organise visits to various holy places and places of worship. The common aspects of teaching of various saints and religious teachers can be discussed. Festivals of various religions and cultures can be celebrated and the significance of each one of them can be discussed. Stories of saints and mythological stories can be discussed to transmit cultural values to the pupils.

Propagation of Scientific Humanism

Teachers should make it clear to the pupils that love for humanity is the best religion. All religious customs should be comprehended with a scientific rational outlook.

Thus, the role of teachers in promoting secularism is mainly to develop spirit of tolerance, bridge the barriers and make the pupils realise the concept of a World Religion which teaches the values of Love, Piety and Kindness to all living beings.

SUMMARY

Role of the teacher in a changing Indian Society

1. **Changing times and complex roles of the teachers.**
2. **Expectations of** - the pupils, the heads of the institutions, the parents, the society and the teachers.
3. **Roles of the teacher** - Co-learner, Friend, philosopher and guide, Director, Animator, Motivator, Facilitator, Administrator, Leader, Evaluator, Researcher, Reformer and Community educator.
4. **Professional Ethics:** The fundamental principles of the professional ethics of the teacher may be classified into Philosophical, Psychological and Sociological principles.

a. *Philosophical principles:* Positive thinking, Life-long learning, Aesthetic sense, Professional integrity, Moral character.

b. *Psychological principles:* Personality of the teacher, Teacher's role in the development of the personality, Teacher asa motivator, Teacher as a counsellor.

c. *Sociological principles*

5. **Demands of Political Ideologies —**

Preamble to our Indian Constitution and the concepts for which youth of the country has to be educated,

Constitutional Provisions pertaining to education,
Problems of National Development,
Education and National Development.

6. **Roles of the teachers with regard to each goal:**

Role of teachers in a Democracy - Professional growth and excellence, Human Resource Development, Democratic Methods, Modernisation, Social Awareness.

Role of teachers in Equality.

Role of teachers in Social Justice.

Role of teachers in Universalisation of Elementary Education.

Role of teachers in Social and National Integration and International Understanding.

Role of teachers in Secularism.

APPENDIX

LINKAGES THAT FACILITATE THE REFORMATIVE AND REHABILITATIVE FUNCTIONS OF TEACHERS

Teachers are responsible for Human Resource Development. In their endeavour to achieve the goal of education, they have to perform many corrective, diagnostic and remedial tasks. These tasks cannot be performed in isolation but they have to form a network in collaboration with a team of medical and paramedical experts, administrative bodies, social and voluntary organisations. Establishing linkages with special organisations and parents will facilitate a co-ordination of efforts, continued interaction and exchange of ideas regarding course of action and the results achieved. The linkages that may be helpful are as follows:

Medical Social Worker

The medical social worker helps in studying the history of health problems of the pupils and the probable impact on the achievement of the pupils and the remedial measures that may be adopted.

Pediatrician

The child specialist may in collaboration with other consultants, give expert medical advice regarding preventive measures and improvement of general health. This can be achieved by periodical medical-check up conducted in the school.

Clinical Psychologist

Certain behaviours may be due to emotional problems which may be deep-rooted and require psychological intervention. In such cases the teacher can seek the advice of a clinical psychologist. The co-ordinated effort of the teacher and the parents in providing a planned objective-based environment will enable the pupil to overcome his problems.

Speech Therapist

Speech defects hamper the reading and oral expression of the child. As a result, the child may develop other psychological problems. Problems in pronunciation, stammering and stuttering may require constant training and follow-up work. The teacher can discuss such problems with the speech therapist and monitor the follow-up and progress of the child with the co-operation of the parents of the child and the other pupils in the class. Such cases generally arise when partially deaf and dumb children are being integrated in the normal school.

Occupational Therapist

Occupational Therapy is useful in cases where neurological defects or illnesses causing brain damage affect the co-ordination and movement of muscles. In such cases, the muscles which are affected need to be re-educated to receive the messages from the brain and act. In order to achieve this, specific activities have to be selected, bearing in mind the stimulation of the particular affected muscles and the psychology of the patient. The defects which have to be treated with occupational therapy are at times mistaken by teachers for carelessness, lack of interest and unwillingness to learn. For instance, a dyslexic patient or dysgraphic patient may be scolded by the teacher for reversing letters in a word or for not writing. Some problems may arise due to problems in vision and hearing. Hence proper diagnosis and follow-up with the correct advice from the occupational therapist is essential. In view of the fact that both the occupational therapist and the teacher are involved in education of the child, it is necessary for both of them to interact and co-ordinate the activities and learning experiences planned for the child's development.

Physiotherapist

In the case of orthopaedically handicapped children who are being integrated into the normal school, the advice of the physiotherapist and follow-up with the help of the Physical Training teacher is useful.

Social and Voluntary Organisations

The teacher has to be in contact with social and voluntary organisations to acquire up-to-date information about the facilities and equipment available for the rehabilitation of the visually and hearing impaired individuals, the financial assistance available and the procedures involved.

Administrative bodies

The Municipal Corporations, the Primary Health Centres and Family Welfare Centres provide assistance in organising and conducting medical check-up, taking up preventive measures to avoid spread of epidemics and providing facilities for immunisation. In fact, these bodies are responsible for maintaining hygienic conditions, clean environment and preventing pollution.

Teachers are the focal points of a network of medical, social and administrative bodies and the society at large - all contributing their resources for Human Resource Development. Teachers have to utilise the appropriate resources and bring about co-operation and co-ordination of functions to build an active society by proper utilisation of human potential in its varying proportions. This means an incessant linkage between teachers, experts of various disciplines, parents and pupils. Besides, teachers are in contact with the child for a longer time and are in contact with the parents. So teachers are the key persons to work in collaboration with the paramedical team, organisations deeply involved in welfare of children like Indian Council for Development of Children (ICDC).

BIBLIOGRAPHY

1. Aggarwal, J.C., Development and Planning of Moden Education, Vikas Publishing House Pvt. Ltd., New Delhi. 1982.
2. Aggarwal, J.C., Teachers Role, Status. Service Conditions and Education in India, A Reference Manual. Doaba House. Delhi, 1988
3. Aggarwal, J.C., Theories and Principles of Education, Vikas Publishing House Pvt. Ltd., New Delhi, 1992.
4. Bhatia, Kamala and Bhatia B.D., Theory and Principles of Education, Doaba House, Delhi, 1992.
5. Chandavarkar, G.N., Maharshie, Karve Popular Prakashan. Bombay, 1958.
6. Dharamvir and Sharma B.P., Socio-Cultural Development, A Global Perspective, New Delhi, 1989.
7. Hanson, John, W. and Brembeck Cole, S., Education and the Development of the Nations, Holt, Rinchart and Winston, U.S.A., 1966.
8. Kim, V., Zaidi, M.H., Guzman De, R.P., Gromchai, P., The Role of the University in National Development - Four Asian Studies. Vikas Publishing House Pvt. Ltd., Delhi, 1980.
9. Lockyer. Norman, Education and National Progress, Mc. Millan and Co., London, 1906.
10. Reuchilin, M., Individual Orientation in Education, Project Volume: Educating Man for the 21st Century, Martinus Nijhof Hague, 1972.
11. Ryans, David G., Characteristics of Teachers, Sterling Publishers (P) Ltd., Delhi, 1969.
12. Taba, Hilda, Curriculum Development, Harcourt, Brace and World Inc., New York, 1962.
13. Walia, J .S., Great Educators, Paul Publishers, Jullundur, 1993
14. Walia, J.S., Principles and Methods of Education, Paul Publishers, Jullundur, 1993.
15. Wheeler. D.K.. Curriculum Process. University of London Press Ltd.. London. 1967.
16. Education on the Move - Extracts from background papers prepared for the Report of the International Commission in the Development of Education. Unesco Press. Delhi. 1975.